MENTOR THEM OR THEY WILL

Expert Advice for Youth Mentors Who Teach Self-Discipline Life Skills

CHAD C. CARMACK, EdD

Learning Pursuit, LLC

Hockessin, Delaware

2024

MENTOR THEM OR THEY WILL

Expert Advice for Youth Mentors Who Teach Self-Discipline Life Skills

ISBN: 978-1-964270-01-2 Trade paper

ISBN: 978-1-964270-02-9 E-book

ISBN: 978-1-964270-00-5 Hardcover

Published 2024 by Learning Pursuit, LLC

Book design and publication: Learning Pursuit, LLC

Copy and line editing: Rebecca Franks

Cover design: Jamie Tipton, Open Heart Designs

Developmental editing: Ella Ritchie, Stellar Communications Houston

Proofreading: Elizabeth Hudgins

https://www.learningpursuit.org

Contents

Preface

It was past midnight when I ran from my friends to the front door of my house. I yelled back to them that I would be right back, then I opened the door quickly and went inside.

I didn't expect to find my father awake. He looked up and scanned me with a questionable look.

The last thing I wanted was a confrontation. Dad had a short temper, so I looked for a way to get through this encounter without trouble. I looked him in the eye and smiled. "Can I borrow one of your shirts?"

Earlier, my friends and I had gone to a party where I became involved in a fight. My opponent almost shredded my shirt, and now I had to explain my predicament to my father.

The situation with my dad happened long ago, but I recall his response, "Why would I lend you a shirt? You were in a fight. I don't want any of my shirts ripped up like that."

His response made perfect sense. The torn shirt was visible, but I also had a torn relationship with my father. He knew my history of making poor decisions as a youth. Why would his answer be anything but no?

Years later, Dad and I would laugh about the situation. I told him he did a good job by not acting as an enabler.

Having a ripped shirt was the least of my worries. As a youth, I gravitated to others who were like me, people who liked having fun and pushing limits. Hypothetically, many of my friends had torn shirts. Hopefully, those people in my past did not go as far as I did in messing up my life.

I don't blame any of my friends for the poor decisions I made in my adolescence. I had the power of choice. I am responsible for my actions.

Because of my lack of self-discipline as a youth, I lost many opportunities. I floundered in work settings, school, athletics, personal health, and family situations. My decision-making was horrible. I created problems that took years to fix.

However, after turning my life around, I became more patient with young people who were headed down the wrong path. I tried harder to help them because I had experience with changing directions in life. I also realized that a few mentors significantly changed my life's path.

Some of you may be interested in mentoring because you're like me and made many mistakes as a youth. Others have a different perspective. But we all have one thing in common: we believe that youth can benefit from our guidance. We want them to avoid problems and have a path to a successful and productive life.

Young people trying to find their way in life need highly effective mentors. Our world is changing fast. Young people must navigate things adults could never have imagined, such as online peer pressure (social media), ever-changing technology, the drug that can kill you the first time tried, endless entertainment, and a growing trend of not experiencing face-to-face interactions. We must move young people out of danger zones or paths to nowhere. Mentors must teach our youth successful life skills like self-discipline. Self-discipline is fundamental to youth development.

What's at stake for youth who need a mentor but don't have one? No one can predict precisely what will happen. I've not stayed in touch with people who were friends in my youth. However, one of my relatives who was with me in my youth has shared examples of tragic outcomes: early death, substance abuse, prison, poor health, lack of life skills, and poverty. As an educator, I saw the same outcomes with youth who had enormous potential.

When I started to mentor others, I learned quickly that the mentor benefits from the relationship as much as the mentee. It's incredibly satisfying to see others succeed.

I mentor youth and adults. In the process of mentoring, I've learned that one of the best ways to reach more youth is to help adults who want to be mentors. Coaching and inspiring adults was critical in my work as a school principal. There is no way one person can do it all.

Our school teams had exceptional student academic achievement successes because of focused attention on planning, instruction, classroom management, educator and student interactions, assessments, and mentoring. My firsthand experiences with educators prepared me to write this book. I have worked with many highly effective teachers, coaches, and mentors.

Several years after my dad caught me coming home with a ripped shirt, I sat in the office of my supervisor, a high-ranking United States Air Force sergeant. I was in trouble again. Like my father, he was a no-nonsense type of person. His words of wisdom as a mentor were words I needed then.

He probably never considered himself a mentor. In fact, he probably doesn't even remember me. However, there is no doubt that he cared about me enough to listen and provide me with excellent advice.

He talked about potential. He gave great examples of how I reminded him of his grandfather. His grandfather made many of the same types of mistakes I was making. I could tell that he greatly respected his grandfather but was sad that his grandfather never utilized his God-given skills.

The sergeant's presentation to me was not spectacular. He just spoke from the heart and gave me hope. Somehow, his words made me look into my future. His words started me on the path to a better life. Now, I only practice fighting skills during martial arts training.

In this book, I share real-world examples to help you as a youth mentor. I hope this will be a book that you continue to return to when you encounter young people lacking self-discipline. When you find yourself with the most challenging mentee, be encouraged to know your efforts may not manifest until years later. Never give up! Keep mentoring our youth.

Respectfully,

Chad C. Carmack

For more information about the author or youth character-building, please visit https://www.learningpursuit.org.

Sign up for our newsletter at https://www.learningpursuit.org/subscribe.

Note: I wrote the stories in this book in good faith from my memory of events. I have changed or combined the names of the people in the stories. The stories are works of fiction or creative nonfiction. Any resemblance to actual persons, living or dead, is purely coincidental.

Chapter 1

Relationships First

As a teacher, I had a student who consistently disrupted my class and was a major challenge. At the time of our teacher-student conflicts, I had no idea that my interactions with this student made a positive impression. I didn't consider the relationship a mentoring situation; I saw it as a constant conflict.

I had high expectations in the classroom. My goal as a teacher was to make sure that student learning was taking place. Teaching and mentoring both require a level of self-discipline and high expectations. Without behavioral expectations, teaching and mentoring will be at risk, and disruptions will likely interfere with your goals. Because of my constant review of expectations, I was confident that students in my classroom knew what I expected. I reinforced and reviewed expectations repeatedly.

Communicating expectations is a large part of the mentoring process. If you don't provide expectations as a mentor, the mentee may not learn fundamental life lessons as you expect.

The student who constantly disrupted my class—I thought he hated me, and I was okay with that. I wasn't in the teaching business to be loved. I wanted students to learn. On any given day, the disruptive student would try to interrupt lessons with erratic behavior. He wouldn't participate in classroom activities, he disturbed other students—he was not meeting my expectations.

I dealt with the problem behavior by using reminders and interventions, preferring subtle approaches whenever I could. For instance, I had private meetings with the student to remind him of my classroom expectations.

I continued to work with him, and eventually, after much effort, he started improving. Though he wasn't particularly happy with my process, I pushed forward with high expectations and did what was best for the learning in the classroom.

Although I saw improvement, other teachers commented that they saw poor behavior in their classes. While I was happy to see his progress in my class, it was discouraging to see how his behavior hurt his relationships with others.

One thing that energized this student was his desire to play sports. He would do the minimum academically so he could pass his classes; but by doing this, he was able to participate in sports. I was also a coach and witnessed his athletic potential. I made an effort to compliment his athletic efforts sincerely. Our teacher-student relationship grew stronger but was far from comfortable and dynamic. He asked to meet with me at the end of his senior year. During our meeting, he confided that he didn't feel prepared for anything beyond high school. I did a lot of listening during that meeting and can't remember giving him any life-changing wisdom, so I was pleasantly surprised when he came to me to ask for advice. By not lowering my expectations for him, we had established a working relationship. He seemed to trust my opinion.

This exchange with my former student reinforced in my mind the importance of relationships. You may be frustrated with your relationship with a mentee. You may believe there is no positive relationship because of strained interactions. But you may be wrong. You may make a difference in a person's life even if you feel things are not going well.

> **Learning Pursuit Pointer #1**
>
> *Even with a challenging start, never underestimate the*
> *profound positive impact mentoring efforts can have*
> *on a young person's life.*

Years later, I was a principal at a middle school and leading a community meeting when I looked up and noticed a young man at the back of the room sitting with a student.

After the meeting, the young man greeted me with a smile. "Do you remember me?" Of course, I remembered him, the student athlete I struggled to connect with years prior. He shared that he was doing well and appreciated my efforts during his high school years.

Now he was the mentor to the young student who accompanied him to the meeting. He introduced him as a family member and shared that he was planning to give his best to the school. He communicated high academic and behavioral expectations and went on to share with the young student that he enjoyed a great relationship with me.

I was extremely honored to continue the relationship that started as a challenge. I felt confident that he was a fantastic mentor and role model for the student.

Even if things start off challenging, don't take your mentoring relationships for granted. Keep your expectations high. You never know when you might make a difference in the life of another.

The Drive to Know Your Mentee

I felt unsafe and at risk. I was driving on a busy highway. There was no way to change to another lane. Since only guardrails were available where I wished I could pull my car over, doing so was not an option. There was nowhere for me to go. My focus was on the traffic in front of me, but I had to continually glance into the rearview mirror. Trouble was right behind me.

Why would I want to get off the road? Behind me was a driver who didn't appear to know she was driving a vehicle. She was intently looking at the cell phone in her hand. I could see in the rearview mirror that her focus was not on driving her two-thousand-pound car at sixty miles an hour. To her, it seemed, the screen on her cell phone was much more important.

For several minutes, I cautiously watched her unsafe and poor driving skills. Time seemed to be moving in slow motion. I knew that if I had to brake quickly, leaning on the horn and braking was my only hope not to be smashed.

You may have had a similar situation. Were there other options? Some would honk the car horn immediately upon seeing the inattentive driver. If I had done that, would she have put her phone down? Would she have gone road-rage crazy? I don't know. I chose to wait for my opportunity to exit the road.

Because I had no relationship or connection at all with the driver, teaching was not an option. Like people on a crowded interstate highway, mentors and mentees who don't have a relationship will struggle with teaching and learning. Just because people are close, doesn't guarantee learning will take place.

I wonder who taught the careless driver to drive with her eyes glued to the phone in her hand? When she learned how to drive, did her teacher build a relationship? Did they teach her the dangers of driving while texting or looking at a small screen instead of the road? The teacher was ineffective because the woman was driving so carelessly. This woman was alone in the car, but what if her driving teacher had been sitting in the passenger seat? Would the teacher have provided her with feedback? If her teacher also drives while looking at a screen, maybe that's why the woman was not effectively monitoring her moving car.

On the other hand, her teacher may have taught her the correct driving skills, but the woman chose to disregard them or just didn't have the self-discipline to drive safely. I saw firsthand that she needed at least a reminder. She needed a teacher.

Highly effective teachers and mentors help mentees learn fundamental principles. They also build relationships that allow them to provide feedback when the mentee drifts from the skills taught.

The inattentive driver has the potential to be in an accident, but what would she learn from the accident? A more productive way to learn is to avoid accidents altogether. A friend could remind her of the dangers on the road. Mentors with good relationships with their mentees can do the same intervention. Friendly reminders help mentees learn and grow.

Because I had no relationship with the careless driver behind me, teaching was out of the question. If I were mentoring her, how would I build a teaching relationship?

It takes time to build a mentor-mentee relationship. My mentors always found time to meet. Even if visits were short, we had meaningful discussions. Those simple efforts to spend time with me helped me grow. Even if a mentor was my supervisor, they had a way of letting me know they were there to help me become more effective.

During visits, the best mentors are very observant. They collect evidence to provide feedback or find ways to start discussions based on what they see. They're not afraid to share paths to improvement. The feedback process is a natural part of mentoring. Providing feedback doesn't have to be some tricky system learned from a book, nor is it a magic formula where the mentor must share two positives for every recommendation. Yes, positive feedback is essential, but authentic feedback from a caring mentor has value. A trusting relationship must include the mentor providing positive feedback as well as feedback for growth.

I discussed this with a teacher who was in a mentoring program. She was frustrated with mandatory meetings with her mentor. The frustration was because the mentor rarely visited the mentee's classroom. The meetings were a mandatory requirement in a mentoring program.

Another frustration was that the mentor rarely provided any feedback. How could the mentor provide feedback if the mentor had never visited the classroom? It was as if the mentor and mentee were going through the motions to fulfill the mentoring regulation. On paper, there was a mentoring program, but in reality, it was an ineffective situation between two people. It was not mentoring. Because the mentor never visited the classroom, the meetings were unproductive. The mentee couldn't grow without feedback. It's no wonder that the new teacher was frustrated with the process. In her eyes, it was a waste of time.

Similarly, I encountered a young driver who simply needed feedback.

They Need Feedback

An inattentive young driver looking at her cell phone was not getting feedback to keep her safe. There was no one in the car to coach her face-to-face.

I like providing in-person feedback. One can misinterpret written feedback or another cue like a car horn, but face-to-face feedback allows opportunities for discussion and clarification. Like the teacher, the driver needed a caring mentor in the car to help.

In addition to spending time helping your mentee grow by providing feedback, looking for a way to measure the effectiveness of your mentoring is essential. Is the relationship working? Is your mentee driving with eyes on the road? Eyes on the road might be a great measure. Observation skills help in the measuring process.

The mentor should evaluate the relationship between the mentor and mentee, and that process must include realistic measurements and opportunities for the mentee to improve. If you're mentoring, what measures will you use to measure success? Providing direction means providing feedback after you observe. You have to share the facts.

For the teacher's mentor, visiting the classroom could be a time to collect evidence like the number of students engaged, instructional time, classroom management procedures, challenge level of teacher questions, and more. For the unsafe driver, a mentor would have to ride along and provide feedback after observing driving behavior.

I was ready for a mistake. The young driver following me was not paying attention. I could have blasted the horn and taken action to alert the driver that she was in danger of hitting my car. I was looking for a quick way to exit the dangerous situation. Later, a friend suggested I could have turned on my emergency flashers. That would have been a fantastic option; but, unfortunately, I didn't think of it at the time. I did survive, though. I exited as soon as I saw an opportunity to leave the road, allowing the young driver to pass.

The learning potential was not evident. The driver didn't gain knowledge of a new skill for safe driving, and I didn't change her behavior in any way. She was not a safe driver at the time of the incident, and when she passed my car, she continued the unsafe pattern. The same may be true for the teacher who never received feedback from an effective mentor program.

Spirited discussion can make a difference. Mentors should be observant of opportunities to share ideas that might save a driver's life or make a teacher more effective. Courageous conversations are encouraged, along with experiences that provide opportunities to discuss outcomes.

Young people should be allowed to try new things and experience life opportunities. Mentors must always be on the lookout for opportunities to initiate real-world experiences. With experience comes a certain amount of risk. As the mentee tries new things and explores new learning opportunities, there is always a chance of failure. Everyone can learn from failure.

Failures come in different sizes. Mentors with experience have usually had their share of failures. The best mentors know that failure is one of the best ways to learn. The wise learn not to make the same mistakes in life. Mentees might not have that same perspective. Some young people fear failure, but we must encourage them to push forward and try new things.

Mentors have an advantage. We sometimes have experience with things in life that it would be wise to avoid. If you notice your mentee moving toward a big problem, warn them. Be up front with them as you identify the problem, tell them what to avoid, and share with them why.

But what happens when the experience turns into a negative or a loss? Teach youth to look at losses as learning opportunities. Explain to them that losing should not be a habit but rather a chance to learn. What should we *not* do in the future? Were there some wins? What else can you learn from the situation? We all fail at times. Successful people learn from the situation and move on to the next opportunity, never letting fear of failure stop them.

It's important to guide your mentee in analyzing a win or loss and to look for information that will be helpful in the future. While evaluating, mentors should listen well. If we teach by talking too much, we miss listening, a key component of building relationships.

When the people we are mentoring don't seem to be able to break down a situation or experience so that they can learn from it, questions become a great teaching tool. There are always opportunities to ask questions strategically. Questions can guide a mentee to an answer or something they may have missed from the learning experience.

I thoroughly enjoy watching others learn through experiences. Real-world experiences seem to create lasting memories. They can teach us the path to success or furnish us with a road map to prevent us from repeating our failures.

Identify Areas of Interest

Building a relationship can be even more challenging when someone else assigns you to a mentee.

In every school where I worked, academic excellence was a written goal and a critical part of the strategic plan. Part of academic excellence is getting students to a proficient level of reading. In addition to regular reading classes, our teams would schedule additional time or supplemental programs to help students achieve reading goals.

As an educator, I wanted to contribute to the school's new reading program, so I volunteered as a mentor and received a student mentee. The assignment was random. Before the programming assignment, I didn't know the student. Through assessment testing, I learned that my newly assigned mentee was below proficiency in reading and not reading on grade level.

One of the first things I did after meeting the student is something I consider a critical part of the mentoring process: I listened to his dreams and goals for the future. I learned that he wanted to improve his academic progress, and he acknowledged that becoming a better reader would help in this area. I wanted him to become excited about the reading process and become a lifelong learner. Our goals were similar.

I also discovered that he was interested in sports and wanted to find ways to become a better athlete. This was helpful information. I was able to share that improvement in sports linked to reading about great athletes.

Teachers can probably relate to my experience. Millions of young school-age youth want to be athletes. Some aspire to be professional athletes. Most teachers will also probably agree that many of the youth who want to be professional athletes don't dream of becoming great writers or readers.

I was not surprised by my mentee's goals. I remember when I was a youth, athletics was a significant focus of my energy. I wish I had had a few teachers or mentors who could have shared how my extracurricular activities linked to reading and writing. They may have improved my academic progress and athletic abilities.

To build a relationship with your mentee, you must first listen. By listening, you can identify areas of interest and areas needing improvement. Ask questions about what they want to learn.

I was assigned to my mentee to help him become proficient in reading, but I don't believe I could have helped by only teaching reading strategies. I had to find a way to motivate him to read. Together, we read books about athletes from a variety of sports.

Those books allowed my mentee to experience the excitement of winning on the sports field. He began to look forward to spending time with me reading books about his athletic heroes. We both enjoyed the time together. Somewhere in the process, he realized he was becoming a better reader. He started to read books outside of our mentor-mentee relationship and was excited to tell me about some of the stories he was reading. I was thrilled to see his improvement and academic success.

I don't believe the relationship would have worked without my finding his interests. As a mentor, don't force your goals on your mentee. Early in the process, try to discover what they want to learn. What will benefit them in the mentor-and-mentee relationship? Without this fundamental principle, the relationship may not work.

The student received me as a mentor because it was an assigned situation. Assigned mentoring cases can be successful with a focus on the relationship. Without that focus, the mentor-mentee relationship will likely falter.

Steer Away from Dangerous Alleys

While meeting with a group of young people, the topic came up of personal safety on city streets that are known for high-crime situations. I knew the discussion participants well. Although young, they demonstrated that they knew how to think through problems and overcome challenges.

We agreed that the behavior of a stranger could be unpredictable. Several of the participants had stories about strange situations on city streets. One youth, who lives in a city neighborhood plagued with criminal activities, shared with the others that he didn't understand why people took chances in the city. He expanded on his comment by sharing a rule based on his life experience: he doesn't venture into unfamiliar city alleys. He knows that more crimes occur in alleys or backstreets in the city. In his mind, based on crime statistics and stories, those areas are dangerous. To avoid what could be a dangerous situation, he simply doesn't venture into the alleys. Like this streetwise young man, if you're aware of problem areas, don't go there. I can confidently say that most of us have experienced or witnessed peers not giving good advice. Unlike the youth who provided the others with information that seemed to make sense, there is always another who is influencing in a bad way and giving poor advice.

While working in corrections and education, I regularly witnessed peers negatively influencing others. Their influence led to problems: drugs, alcohol, crime, gangs, poor academic achievement, and more.

When we mentor, we need to find ways to communicate "danger ahead" situations. We can guide young people away from impending mistakes, problems, safety issues, and obstacles. Our mentee should get good advice from us because they may not get it from their peers.

Taking on challenges and trying new things is undoubtedly an excellent way to learn. We can learn from our mistakes. But guidance and coaching our mentee away from big problems is a part of the mentoring job description.

Even with experience, a life skill reminder can be worthwhile. Reminders help us to recall previous mistakes and lessons learned.

Years before hearing the young person's advice about back alleys, I visited a community center one day in my role as a principal of an inner-city school. Parking was always a challenge when I went to the community center. After finding a parking spot, I walked to the center using the sidewalks on the main streets. After the meeting, I decided to use a long back alley as a shortcut back to my car. Although I didn't see anybody in the alley, it felt like a bad idea. The area was shielded from the view of pedestrians on the main street by rundown buildings. I was an easy target.

Later, a colleague and friend who grew up in that area confirmed that I had made a wrong decision by walking down the alley and taking a shortcut without knowing the neighborhood. From that point on, I stopped venturing into areas with which I was not familiar. My colleague had become my teacher, and he reinforced what I learned from my walk through a back alley.

As mentors, we should look for opportunities to provide experiences and teach. Mentees will benefit from both.

Unlike my colleague, who was demonstrating friendship when he graciously shared information, some people might not be as giving. We must be gracious and take advantage of teaching opportunities. As we work with mentees, our charge is to creatively share knowledge. Superior mentors balance listening and teaching.

Don't go there can mean more than physically being in a location. As mentors, we can steer our mentees away from dangerous situations: drugs and alcohol, bad friendships, gangs, criminal activity, technology addictions, and other life-changing situations youth may encounter.

As we plan our mentoring teaching objectives, we have an opportunity to develop leaders rather than followers. Youth with leadership training have a better chance of not going with the crowd. Remember, if we don't mentor them, they will. *They* could be any number of people who have a negative influence. People with bad influence could be other youth or adults. We need to have the most significant influence over our mentees.

Some youth are lucky. The lucky ones have parents and mentors to show and teach life skills. Having different experiences can become an opportunity to practice leadership, creativity, decision-making, planning, and more. Other youth are not so lucky and may have observed leadership skills from those with distorted values and destructive character.

I consider leadership a must-learn life skill. Mentors who are leaders and teach leadership skills can have a tremendous impact on young people.

Chapter 2

Principles, Values, and Outcomes

The military changed my life in large part because of its mandatory organizational self-discipline requirements. I joined the United States Air Force because I wanted to serve my country. However, what I received was perhaps far greater: the gift of self-discipline. Before enlisting, I didn't realize I was missing out on fundamental self-discipline principles.

Before my military service, I knew some self-discipline principles but didn't implement those skills into daily life. The military has a system to instill values and teach principles for success. They made us take action, which allowed us recruits to see that the principles work.

What did I learn in the military? Here are only a few self-discipline components that the military taught me: self-control, firmness of purpose, willpower, determination, restraint, endurance, lifelong learning, thinking before you act, and finishing what you start. These are just a few.

As you mentor, remember that you can provide youth with skills they can use throughout their lives. Military training instructors do the same in a compressed amount of time.

Military leaders know there is no typical high school student. Each person comes to basic training with different values based on community, family, upbringing, friends, and other influences. They may or may not have learned success principles relating to leadership, teamwork, and work ethics. Individual recruits may not understand value systems.

Individuals and groups establish values, and values can evolve. A person's values depend on experiences and their unique perspective. Every person looks at the world differently based on individual influences.

My academic life in high school was structured around the sports I played and my goal of going to college. It was vital for me to get good grades so I could participate in sports. I had to make time to study and prepare for classes, and I put in the minimum time required to get passing grades.

My mother and father expected me to receive passing grades, but I don't recall my family discussing the value and applications of learning. I was not highly self-disciplined in the process of learning, and I don't remember focusing on the real-world application of learning.

I knew that I had to get a good SAT score and have good grades to go to college, so at least I had that standard. Although I didn't realize it, I had a value structure as a high school student. Self-discipline helped me get the results I needed to get into college, but it didn't keep me there. I dropped out before finishing.

Before being accepted into the military, my self-discipline and values were far from fine-tuned. The United States Air Force helped me with that problem. They jumpstarted me into a brand-new value structure.

The value structure of the military demanded self-discipline, and the training involved requires a self-discipline mindset that applies to things both big and small. The new value system of the military, which I began to learn right away, is this: the military family.

On one day during my immersion into a new value system, everything seemed to be going well. I was in the middle of some small cleaning detail in the barracks, doing my best to meet the expectation, which was perfection. The training instructors were ready to point out loudly anything that was substandard.

I was mentally relaxing while doing the work. All that abruptly ended as I heard one of my instructors screaming out my name and order, "Carmack! Get over here now!"

I sprinted around the corner to where he was standing. I was sure I had done something wrong because rarely does something go right when a sergeant is yelling at you in basic training. When I reached the training instructor, he stood next to my bed. With him was the dorm chief. The dorm chief was a recruit who was in a leadership position and assisted the training instructors. I had a great relationship with the dorm chief, and I could tell from his facial expression that he wasn't sure what was coming next.

The training instructor hovered over me and moved in close. Though he was glaring and appeared to be unhappy, I tried not to show any emotion. He started yelling comments about my clothing. I had neatly folded the clothing and had it stacked near the bed.

He screamed at me, "What do you see?" He was pointing toward the folded clothing, and I knew that there was no correct answer. I answered that I saw my folded clothing. My observation skills didn't seem to satisfy him.

He quickly redirected his gaze and attention to the dorm chief and started to move in that direction. If something goes wrong with the other recruits, it isn't just the recruits' problem—the dorm chief is responsible. When you're the leader, you're responsible for the results.

He asked the same question to the dorm chief: "What do you see?" The dorm chief shared that he also saw folded clothing. "I have never seen shirts folded this well!" said the training instructor. He looked at me. "You need to teach others how to do this!"

The dorm chief looked closely at the folded clothing and answered, "Yes. I agree, Sergeant."

The training instructor, dorm chief, and I were in a different world from when I was in high school. My parents never expected precision clothing folding. I put my clothing away as a kid, but I never had to be perfect. I don't recall my parents teaching me the right way to fold a T-shirt.

Everything became important during basic training. We had to do the little things right to ensure the significant actions would get done correctly. There was a belief that if you demonstrated discipline and took care of insignificant jobs, you had a better chance of completing the big mission, which included more complicated activities.

I was surprised when the training instructor started to yell throughout the barracks that he had never seen clothing folded so perfectly. Looking back, I'm positive that he was exaggerating and performing; however, he was making a point to me and the other recruits.

After pointing out that he felt I could fold clothing well, he shared that I was now an element leader. An element leader works to help the dorm chief by leading a small group. He promptly fired the airman who was the element leader before me. The training instructor didn't explain why, but all recruits saw the previous element leader make many mistakes. Training instructors didn't make it a habit of confidentially reprimanding those of us training. If you made mistakes, everyone knew about it.

I knew that I had to lead and not make mistakes that would hurt the small group for which I was responsible. This was a perfect time for me to focus on leadership principles.

Principles are fundamental truths, unwavering and robust. Principles stay the same over time. We can depend on the stability of a principle.

Learning Pursuit Pointer #2

Principles are fundamental truths, unwavering and robust. Principles stay the same over time. We can depend on the stability of a principle.

Below are a few leadership principles I learned while serving as an element leader:

- The people you lead are watching you. If you expect self-control, you must be in control of your behavior.

- If you're the leader, you must have a firm purpose. You must lead by example. Team members will support your firmness of purpose, but they must first understand why.

- People will not follow leaders who don't demonstrate determination.

- When you start something, finish it. The habit of finishing what you start can be contagious.

The social standards established in basic training required me to adjust my value system. My values had changed from a civilian perspective to an airman in the United States Air Force. Principles of self-discipline had remained the same but were now visible to me. I now had a new self-discipline mindset to get results.

The mission of the United States Air Force is this: "To fly, fight, and win—airpower anytime, anywhere." To complete the mission, Air Force personnel must participate in a shared value system. Supervisors were constantly teaching and reteaching leadership self-discipline principles. Recruits had to demonstrate new standards of self-discipline for future success. Self-discipline principles and values of excellence were the best ways to get desired results.

Building on Principles

I remember walking through many houses when I searched for a home to purchase. It's funny how a few of the homes have vividly remained in my mind. In one house, the hallway slanted approximately fifteen degrees. In the basement of another house, I touched the concrete foundation and watched as it crumbled to white dust. I did not purchase those homes. Their foundations were not stable.

The foundation system is a structure that connects the building to the ground. It's below the first-floor construction. Builders are familiar with elements of a typical foundation: slab, piers, columns, joists, footing, and foundation wall. For architectural engineers, the foundation system represents one of the most important parts of a structure. Without a good foundation, structural problems will occur.

Building foundations is complicated and requires skilled carpenters to ensure the foundation system matches the architectural plan.

The structure above the foundation isn't the only important consideration of the foundation system type. Builders build foundations on soil or ground, which is also critical. If you build a foundation on sand or a shifting type of soil, you can imagine the outcome. When the storms come, the structure will be at risk. Architectural engineers know how important it is to get the foundation built in the right location and ensure the soil under the foundation is stable.

There are some fundamental principles of foundations. Architects secure structures with foundations. Foundations that are not properly built are at risk. The same is true for young people who don't have foundational principles and values.

Architectural engineers receive specific training on how to build functional foundations. They want a foundation to spread the structural weight evenly. Although all buildings settle, the goal is for the foundation to anchor the structure to the ground. In addition, leveling the foundation is a fundamental building skill. Most of us would not appreciate our home leaning like the Tower of Pisa. What happens if the builders and architects don't implement the fundamentals while building? Do improperly built foundations yield consequences? Here are a few results associated with a building's foundation problem:

- Cracks on the interior or exterior of your home

- Doors and windows separated from the brick

- Rotting wood

- Nails popping out of the drywall

- Walls pulling away from the house

- Structural leaning problems

No homeowner wants the problems above. There can't be shortcuts while building the foundation. Architects and builders need to be aware of foundation truths—building principles.

How do principles and values fit into my foundation metaphor? Principles will represent the soil underneath the foundation. Architects and geological engineers depend on science and principles associated with soil or ground. They need to build the foundation with care. By ignoring the principles of building, the house's structure might be in danger.

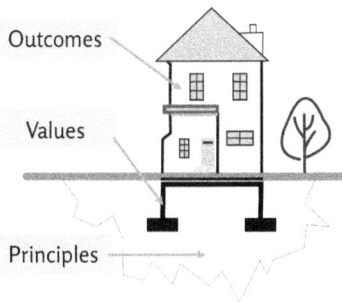

FIGURE 2.1. Principles will represent the soil underneath the foundation. Principles are fundamental truths, unwavering and robust. We can depend on the stability of a principle.

Just like a principle, the soil is like a fundamental truth and has physical laws. There is a science to the soil. Engineers and scientists have developed categories of soil types. They use the categories when determining where to build a foundation and structure. Architects know that the soil will be essential to the outcome. Without stability from soil that will distribute the weight of the house, the structure will be at risk: cracks, sinking, or even collapse can occur.

Loam is a fantastic soil for support of the foundation. Sand, silt, and clay combine to make loam. It's a type of soil that crumbles to the touch, but it's excellent for supporting foundations. It balances evenly and maintains a water balance.

What about clay? The makeup of clay allows for the storage of water. It has many tiny particles. Because of this, it can expand or contract depending on the moisture level. Clay is poor soil for support.

Similarly, without guiding principles, things in society fall apart. Chaos can occur if you ignore basic principles. When I share a principle in this book, picture it underneath the supporting values and outcomes.

Mentors who understand the connection between principles, values, and outcomes will have a teaching advantage. We need an advantage when dealing with young people struggling with self-discipline problems.

Chapter 3

Central Control and Choosing Influencers

As a school principal, I had the opportunity to work with one young man who was an exceptional athlete. He stood out from others on the football field. I built a relationship and was able to get to know him.

One day we had a conversation about his community and home. I shared with him how proud I was that he was succeeding academically and as an athlete. His future looked bright, and he decided to enroll in college. I was so happy to hear about his plan.

He was ready for college, which included completing the college application process. He did this without strong support at home or in his community. He lived in a part of town known for violence. Even though he was a super athlete, he expressed his concern about going home. His routine was to get off the athletic activity bus and go straight for his house door. Once secured behind the door, he didn't come out until the next day to go to school. He didn't want to be involved in any negative situations in his community. He made good choices, and those choices were a part of his plan for future success.

In contrast, he made a conscious effort to surround himself with teachers he respected and coaches who helped to provide him with leadership skills. He didn't randomly choose his mentors. And they were not selected by his family members. He knew that he could make the best decision and controlled who might be his best teachers for success in life. He spent time with those mentors and learned as much as possible.

We Have Control over Who Influences Our Life

Inside the prison was an official work area called Central Control, an essential part of the prison. The person assigned to Central Control worked inside a glass room, and one of his responsibilities was to unlock gates. Massive metal gates circled the glass room. The glass was bulletproof and could withstand prisoner attacks from outside.

The only way to come through a door was for the person in Central Control to hit the button that unlocked the door. Prisoners and correctional officers were not moving if the Central Control officer didn't engage the electronic door lock.

To work in Central Control, you had to learn the rules governing the gates. There were gates around the control room and gates deeper in the prison building. By video and intercom, the central controller monitored gates not directly around the control room. You could open one gate at a time. After a gate was secure, the central controller could open another gate. During any time of a routine day, but especially in an emergency, numerous people requested gate entry. It was a stressful job filled with decision-making linked to the safety and security of others.

Let's use the idea of a central control-type room as a metaphor for choosing mentors and influencers. Each of us has experiences and people who influence us. Some of what we learn from influencers can last a lifetime. For this metaphor, you're the person in central control. Consider someone who comes through a gate as an influencer. You have some control over who transitions through a gate or influences your life.

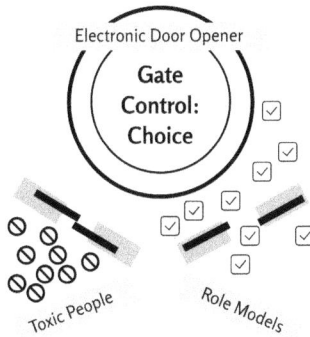

FIGURE 3.1. Let's use the idea of
a central control-type room as a
metaphor for choosing mentors and
influencers.

Many young people might not be aware that they have control over this part of life. As mentors, we should tell them. A goal for our youth should be to increase the influencer's positive gifts of experiences and wisdom. Wisdom will lead to success. A good mentor can also help the mentee to decrease negative situations they find themselves in.

Behind one gate might be family members. Some family members are incredibly giving and provide us with lifelong lessons for success. Other family members might be toxic and provide us with a painful perspective. We can make a choice to keep toxic people out, knowing they will not be effective mentors. Another gate might be considered the gate of friends. Just like family members, friends can be poisonous or help us through life in a positive way. Whether positive or negative, those experiences received from the influencers coming through the gates help shape our value system and how we see our world.

Imagine a youth working behind the glass in central control. They look out at the many gates and people behind the gates. We can categorize the people behind the gates as potential mentors or not: parents, coaches, family, neighbors, teachers, spiritual leaders, and community leaders.

A parent will come through the family gate. In most cases, the youth will have no control over the gate opening. Like the central controller opening a gate for colleagues, youth will open the gate for a parent. The parent is an influencer, and their influence could be positive or negative.

In addition to youth making decisions about influencers, parents and mentors should assist in connecting youth with appropriate influencers and mentors—keeping people out or helping to get them through the door. In other words, our mentee isn't alone in central control. A parent can influence what happens in central control. When a parent isn't available, a mentor is needed.

Parents come with a vast ability to influence their children. Most parents provide direction and do everything possible to guide their children to future success.

Parents have a primary job: to affect their children positively. Whether intentional or not, children learn life lessons from their parents.

Sometimes youth influence can come from small interactions. It's incredible to me the number of times a youth or one of my children will tell me how a particular situation influenced them. At the time, the situation seemed uneventful. Children are watching their parents. As they watch, they learn.

Youth Should Search for Adult Mentors

Youth have more than the central control parent gate. There are so many other gates that can provide opportunities for learning. Behind some of the gates are mentors with life experiences worth more than can be measured.

Teachers, spiritual leaders, family members, community members, coaches, and friends all provide opportunities for our youth. Youth may not realize they can unlock the gates—they are central controllers. Adults need to alert them and guide them to the best influencers. When they find mentors, youth should press the button, open the gate, and start learning. The parent should be a part of the process.

A few weeks before I left for college in 1978, I worked for a small-business owner. We had a very good relationship, and I trusted him and his perspectives.

He was a significant influence as I observed his work ethic. He owned a small farm and hired me occasionally to help with the physical labor. I enjoyed my time with him. He led by example. No one worked harder than him.

He was a natural teacher who noticed when people needed advice. He was straight to the point: "When you get to college, keep your nose clean."

It was his way of communicating that I needed to be responsible. I'm not sure if he knew about my hell-raising as a youth or just knew that most young men need straightforward guidance. Either way, he cared enough about me to give me advice.

To this day, I appreciate his efforts. Now, I advise young people transitioning to a new life challenge.

Learning Pursuit Pointer #3

To find highly effective mentors, we must learn the rules governing the "influencer gate." Make good choices when bringing mentors into your life.

I often share the importance of finding at least one adult mentor. We must be alert to people demonstrating character, expertise, and leadership. I make them understand that they have the power of choice. They must proactively find a mentor—they control the central control influencer gate.

If they listen, some will find a teacher who can mentor them in successful strategies and how to become the best in their field of study. Others might find a highly effective technician who can guide them to higher career levels. Some have shared that they developed higher levels of self-identity by finding spiritual leaders to mentor them.

It isn't up to me to choose their adult mentor. But it's important for youth to find an adult mentor.

I wish I had listened more to the small-business owner who cared enough about me to share advice. I appreciate his words of wisdom and strategy for advising young people.

For youth not transitioning to college or career, a parent should help them in central control to find influencers to let through the gates. They, with the help of their parent, have control.

I had a conversation with a friend who shared his strategy for making sure that his children learned from others. He intentionally identified several adults that he trusted would influence his kids. He made sure those influencers were in the lives of his children. I feel this is a remarkably positive strategy. Without his guidance, his children might not have had opportunities to learn from their chosen mentors.

Taking this idea one step further, I believe it's essential for youth to understand that sometimes they control who they let through a mentoring gate. Youth may have to search for adult mentors beyond the visible gate. The central controller had to monitor gates not directly outside of the glass barrier. Gates deep in the correctional facility were still under their control.

Sometimes mentors feel that they are alone in the mentoring job. We are not alone. Parents will always be a part of the mentoring process. They are the primary influence and our partner. Together we can be influential in the life of a young person. We must help them understand that they will need mentors throughout their lifetime, and they must be proactive and find highly effective mentors. If they don't know that they are in control—like the controller in central control—they may miss out on the tremendous learning opportunities.

Chapter 4

Mentor Quality

L et us consider leadership and character attributes to demonstrate how mentors can be very different. As a mentor, you should constantly look for ways to improve your skills so you can serve youth. Mentors must also look for other people who can influence youth. Using a chart or matrix, we can categorize a mentor by their ability to lead and their character attributes.

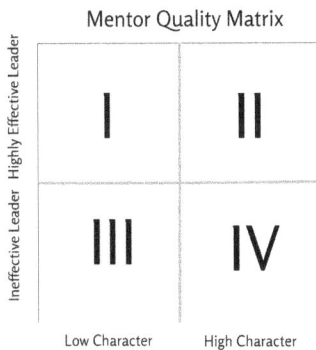

Mentor Quality Matrix

	Low Character	High Character
Highly Effective Leader	I	II
Ineffective Leader	III	IV

FIGURE 4.1. Using a chart or matrix, we can categorize a mentor by their ability to lead and their character attributes.

The matrix has two axes. The *x* axis will compare the level of perceived character from low to high. The *y* axis will communicate the effectiveness of the leader.

Character will be more complicated to chart than leadership effectiveness. You may not see another's true character. However, we can use the information available through direct interactions. Are they honest? Do they follow through on promises? What behaviors lead you to believe the person has good or bad character? I look for evidence like the following:

- Goodness

- Correct behavior

- Good sense of right and wrong

- Courage

- Honesty

- Loyalty

- Good habits

The left part of the *x* axis will designate low character based on the available evidence. The higher character is to the right on the *x* axis.

The bottom of the *y* axis will indicate low effectiveness as a leader. The top of the *y* axis will show highly effective leadership.

Quadrant I Leader

In prison, some prisoners demonstrate high levels of excellence in leadership. Those same leaders have very low character. As a correctional officer, I met many quadrant I leaders. Quadrant I of the Mentor Quality Matrix describes a highly effective leader with low character.

Working as a correctional officer was impactful on my life. You had to learn quickly. I had to deal with difficult people daily. I also had an opportunity to observe incarcerated people demonstrating leadership. Many prison leaders were on the low-character part of the Mentor Quality Matrix.

Most of the leaders in the prison wanted to be invisible. It was not beneficial to them to be constantly followed by correctional officers. They didn't market their leadership skills.

We still found ways to identify the leaders. Sometimes, we learned about leadership activities through other inmates, often called "snitches." At other times, inmates accidentally shared information, which provided us with evidence of leadership.

I always enjoyed trying to find out more about prison leaders because it helped me perform my duties and keep team members safe. We and the inmate leaders were operating in a violent and chaotic environment.

Chaos was known to happen in a large holding area called a block. The block housed forty to fifty inmates. My supervisor assigned me to the block when I first talked to an inmate named Mark.

Mark was one of the toughest inmates in the prison. I never observed any other inmates bothering Mark. He was intelligent, but he was in a gang. The gang was like an insurance policy. If you mess with one person in the gang, you're messing with the whole gang.

I was once at the back of the block, and Mark was sitting at one of the community tables. No one else was around.

Out of curiosity, I asked him, "Who are you afraid of in this prison?"

Without hesitation, he responded, "Rudy!" He seemed sincere.

"Rudy! You have to be kidding me!"

Mark was at least 6'2" and 220 pounds. He was muscular and looked intimidating. On the other hand, Rudy could not have weighed more than 160 pounds. I shook my head in astonishment.

"How is that possible? Rudy?"

Mark looked at me and patiently shared simple details I didn't know. "Rudy is a leader. He supports us and leads by example. When he puts his mind to something, he gets it done. Everyone knows that Rudy has power in this place."

Then he added, "Rudy will kill you without thinking. While others delay in violence, he acts with speed and usually a weapon. In here and on the street, he is a feared leader."

Looking back, I'm sure that Mark was speaking from the heart. I don't know why he shared that information with me, but I started watching Rudy closely. Rudy was low-profile; he never stood out in a crowd. He was extremely smart and creative, and he seemed to lack empathy. There's no doubt he used all skills to lead.

Does a person like Rudy, someone who can easily injure or kill another person, fall into the area of low character? I believe so.

Learning Pursuit Pointer #4

People with high moral character have a sense of right and wrong and do what is right.

My example of a person in quadrant I is extreme but has some value. We should watch for and avoid having quadrant I people mentoring our youth. Though they may be highly effective leaders, they lack character.

A mentor in quadrant I might effectively get short-term results as a leader. With that said, long-term results may be problematic because of low character. Remember, Rudy was in jail.

People with character have a sense of right and wrong and do what is right. The quadrant I mentor doesn't do this. The quadrant I leader may also be self-focused, contributing to relationship problems. Think of the leader who appears to be on top but then loses it all because of some ethical problem. That leader qualifies for quadrant I. A quadrant I leader is not a quality mentor.

Quadrant III Leader

Quadrant III describes an ineffective leader with low character. When I facilitate leadership workshops, most of the participants often have been able to identify at least one boss in their lives who easily fits into this category. When mentoring youth, we must teach effective leadership and character life skills so our youth never become quadrant III leaders.

I've been lucky to have had many highly effective bosses with character. Unfortunately, there were a few I would put into quadrant III of the Mentor Quality Matrix.

While in the Air Force, one of my duties was at Patrick Air Force Base in Florida. It was a fantastic location, and I took advantage of the beach while off duty. However, Florida has some swampy areas that are home to venomous snakes and alligators. When I think of venomous snakes, I think of an experience forced on me by a quadrant III leader.

Our security team had many capable supervisors, but one of our supervisors, Sergeant Weakstone, always seemed to be challenged with his leadership ability. Sergeant Weakstone was most interested in being liked.

Crime was a problem in the area that surrounded our base, and drug dealers were prevalent and wreaked havoc in the community. Our security team had to keep our base secure from criminal activity; and because of the high-level security assets on our base, we had zero tolerance for intruders.

One night, I was working a midnight shift in a location close to the base's perimeter. Sergeant Weakstone's call came through my handheld radio: "We have a breach in our perimeter! I need all airmen to be on the lookout for drug dealers who have come onto our base! This is not a drill!" Adrenaline coursed through my body. Since I was so close to the perimeter of the base, I visually scanned for intruders.

The sergeant began to call out directions to various airmen. He was moving individuals to different areas on the base. I listened closely and took note of team member locations. As he gave orders over the radio, his transmissions began to sound less urgent. I picked up something different in his voice. It was as if he were enjoying the problem. My gut feeling was something wasn't right.

Over the radio, I asked Sergeant Weakstone, "Please confirm that this is not a drill."

He responded, "This is not a drill! Again, this is not a drill!" He continued to call out commands on the radio.

He moved many team members by radio. But I was surprised when he called me. "Airman Carmack! The intruders were approximately one hundred yards in front of your location!"

I was hidden and protected by a vehicle engine as cover. I had a perfect view of the perimeter. The area in front of me was swampy flatland full of Florida wildlife, including venomous snakes.

I could see the swampy area and perimeter easily. Even though it was the middle of the night, the grounds and base perimeter were well lit. "I don't see the intruders." I shared with Sergeant Weakstone. Again, my gut was speaking to me. Something didn't seem right. I asked Sergeant Weakstone again, "Please confirm that this is not a drill."

"This is not a drill. Run as fast as you can over the flatland to the perimeter."

What? His order was not logical. He was telling me to leave my location of cover and concealment. The swampy flatland would make me an easy target for anyone near the perimeter. In addition, I couldn't get the snakes out of my head.

I made sure my rifle was ready to fire and began to crawl across the field. I was crawling fast, but I guess I wasn't crawling fast enough. I heard the sergeant come across the radio, "Senior Airman Carmack! Where are you?"

"I am on the way."

"I can't see you! I need you there immediately! Stand up and run!"

I would be an easy target if armed drug dealers were at the perimeter. I was also at risk of being bitten by a venomous snake. I stood and ran low to the ground in a zigzag pattern across the field. When I reached the perimeter, Sergeant Weakstone called to all team members across the radio, "The drill is over. Nice job, team!"

The sergeant was a quadrant III leader, and he had put our team in danger. He didn't seem to realize the difference between what was right and what was wrong.

Our team had ready-to-use weapons, and we were prepared to defend our base. Sergeant Weakstone shared later that he wanted the drill to be realistic. For this reason, he didn't alert us that the activities were a training drill. His actions caused an extremely risky situation. He hadn't been honest with us, and his actions were inappropriate. This type of behavior was why we didn't respect him as a leader. On the bright side, I didn't get bitten by a snake or shot at by armed drug dealers.

The quadrant III leader will be ineffective as a leader and will demonstrate low character. They may have no record of accomplishing short- or long-term goals, yet they may tell you stories of success. The quadrant III leader is not a good match for a young person looking for guidance.

Quadrant IV Leader

Quadrant IV of the Mentor Quality Matrix describes an ineffective leader who has high character. Although they operate on ethical guiding principles, qualities that make them a good fit for mentoring, they have no or few examples of leadership effectiveness.

When I was ten years old, I thought I was a leader. I was older than my neighbors, so I was in charge.

Throughout my young life, both of my grandmothers spent much time working on my character. They did an excellent job of keeping me in line.

Grandma Esther Poper ensured I was with her on Sunday mornings at church. Following church, she always served family lunch. Around the kitchen table, Grandma Poper was a teacher. She worked hard to build my character by teaching real-world life skills.

Grandma Kathleen (Kitty) Carmack worked on my character by constantly focusing my attention on right and wrong. She was a loving but firm teacher. There were consequences when I made mistakes, but she used my mistakes to teach me about being responsible and good.

With those types of teachers and loving family members, at just ten years old, I had a high character level. They had prepared me well, yet I must not have been paying attention because I didn't learn their leadership skills.

Although unprepared to lead, I took on the responsibility with a group of my neighborhood friends. We were playing outside when we saw the axe and logs just waiting to be split. The axe was magnetic! I immediately ran to it and saw an opportunity for fun. It was going to be fun to lead my neighbors in a lesson on how to chop wood.

If you're a leader, experience is your friend. I didn't have any experience using an axe. That didn't stop me from trying to teach my neighbors how to use an axe to chop wood.

I was doing a fantastic job of describing how to strike through a log powerfully. Since there was a pile of logs, their eyes lit up. I could tell that they were anxious to start chopping. But first, I had to teach them.

I explained, "With power, you can split a log with one strike of the axe!"

I told them to back up as I raised the large axe above my head. With two hands clutching the long handle, I powered the blade toward the log. It split perfectly, but I made a mistake. The axe went through the wood and stuck quite nicely in my foot. I forgot to tell my team how important it is not to have your foot or any other part of your body in the blade's path. I felt discomfort from the axe blade stuck in my foot and my embarrassing situation as a young leader.

I had to get stitches in my foot and learned an important lesson about leading the group: if you lead and teach specific skills, you should know those skills. I was a quadrant IV leader on the day of the axe accident. Thank goodness no one else was injured.

A quadrant IV mentor will not have the skill to show a young person how to become a leader. They may just be starting a career and need more leadership experience. They still will have great qualities, which will benefit the youth. In addition to limited leadership skills, they may have chosen not to participate as a leader. Some people in this quadrant might decide to avoid taking the risk of being placed in leadership positions. People in this quadrant can be great team members.

If you're searching for a mentor who can provide leadership skills, a quadrant IV mentor will not be the perfect fit.

Quadrant II Leader

A quadrant II leader is the type of mentor that we should strive to find and be. A quadrant II leader on the Mentor Quality Matrix describes one who has high character and proven leadership effectiveness. Their behaviors and skills are worth duplicating. This type of leader will have a record that shows short- and long-term results as a leader. They will also have experiences that have allowed them to demonstrate and coach others in learning leadership skills. The best mentors can teach those skills and guide mentees to success.

I am not going to share with you an example of a quadrant II leader. Instead, think about people in your past. Who were the people who demonstrated highly effective leadership? After identifying those leaders, prioritize the list. Who stands out when you consider character?

Each of us has most likely experienced working with a quadrant II leader. These leaders are special. As mentors, we should all strive to be in this category.

Quadrant II mentors know they can make choices that will affect an organization and personal success. They will make challenging, unpopular decisions; however, they do the right thing. This type of leader knows how to build relationships. After all, you can't lead without others wanting to follow. Quadrant II mentors seem to have the formula for a successful life and proven leadership.

To prepare youth for success, we all must be aware of the opportunities mentorships bring. If observant, people searching for mentors can find quadrant II leaders.

Chapter 5

Planning

Teach young people how to plan. Planners get things done. When young people make planning a habit, they can achieve great success.

Use your mentoring skills to hook your mentee creatively. Your hook might be a story of how you found planning a valuable tool to guide you through achieving goals. The goal is for youth to understand how planning links to success.

During one season of my life, I enjoyed my role serving as an assistant football coach. I assisted a competent, competitive team with a coaching staff responsible for a winning mentality. Weekly planning was a part of the process of developing impressive outcomes for the team.

Assistant coaches had a variety of responsibilities. One of my duties was to film Friday night football games. Game films were a historical record and were used to support weekly plans. After I delivered a video of the football game, it allowed us to see how we did and use the measurements and data to help players and the team.

One night while I was filming our team, another scouting coach was sitting in another stadium watching a football game between two other teams. When collecting scouting information, filming the other teams was not permitted. Instead, the coach would frantically take notes. The notes were a measure to get information about teams that would someday be our opponents.

Like looking at the film after the football game, the scouts looked for various observable activities on the football field. We were able to identify the talent, problems, and team strategy. What did the coach do in certain situations? Were there any standout players? Were there any weaknesses, such as players who didn't appear to contribute effectively to the team? Those weaknesses might be areas we could take advantage of in upcoming weeks during our game. All the information was vital to the planning process.

To share our data collection results, we would have coaches' meetings and meetings with the players. During these meetings, we reviewed the film and all data collected. A thorough performance review was a part of the planning process. We had to get ready for the upcoming week of practice and games. To do this, looking back helped us look ahead.

Many teams schedule a time to look at film and review scouting reports. The best teams use measurements from the film and scouting reports to determine how the team and players can improve and win the next game.

We set goals for each upcoming game. We took it one week at a time and built plans based on our performance strengths and weaknesses. Juxtaposition skills were critical as we reviewed our team's and opponent's strengths and weaknesses. We would use the knowledge of their skill level and coaching patterns to take advantage of them. Planning was a way to facilitate victory. We wanted to win.

Although the overall mission was to get as many wins as possible through the season, this weekly planning helped us achieve our desired result.

Learning Pursuit Pointer #5

Priorities, leadership, accountability, and new directions are important components of a plan (PLAN).

Like the coaching staff, youth can use the same evaluation evidence in weekly planning. How did the week go? What needs to change in the upcoming week? How will you make sure those adjustments take place? Were unaccomplished goals important? Maybe they should not be in the plan if they're not necessary.

You may not have a team of coaches helping with the planning process as a mentor. However, a mentor can become incredibly important in this process. Check in to make sure that the mentee is using the plan. Discuss how the planning process is moving along. These types of discussions will benefit the young planner. With guidance, one can fine-tune a skill until it becomes a habit.

Priorities, Leadership, Accountability, and New Directions are important components of a plan (PLAN).

P — Priorities

Priorities become actionable through the planning process. Taking action on the essential planning targets can mean the difference between getting things done or not.

It takes time to prioritize. Setting aside time for planning improves the opportunity for success. Make it a habit to schedule time for planning.

Focus and awareness of what you want in the future helps prioritize. What will be the result? Visualize what benefits will come from taking action. Also, remember what will happen if you don't take action on the actionable targets.

Setting priorities requires not letting less important activities get in the way. Self-discipline helps keep you focused on getting results. Fight for the time needed to get it done. But understand that there will always be interruptions and other forces that compete for your time.

Prioritizing is a fundamental part of the planning process. We mentors can model using self-discipline to accomplish planning skills, such as prioritizing. Our mentees will notice.

L — Leadership

Would you like for your mentee to be a leader or follower? Most likely, you're like me and hope they will be aspiring leaders. We must communicate clearly that highly effective leaders plan.

When I observe highly effective leaders in action, they all seem to practice self-discipline. Also, leaders look to the future and visualize it. Planning separates highly effective leaders from others. They can see into the future and know that it will take self-discipline to plan to make the vision a reality.

If a leader knows the skill of planning is essential, they must demonstrate self-discipline to accomplish it. Planning is vital, so having the self-discipline to make it a part of their life skills will pay off. Regular planning will require willpower. Those who have willpower can fight through inaction.

Not being disciplined can become a comfortable state of being. But when helpful routines become a part of a person's life, there is a reward. Getting past inaction is a type of willpower that accompanies self-discipline.

Connecting leadership and planning might be enough to get our mentees to plan.

A — Accountability

Accountability accompanies planning. A written plan is a promise to yourself. When a person makes a promise, there should be an understanding of responsibility. The planner must evaluate their effort to accomplish the plan. After writing an actionable item at a specific time, a planner must ask what the outcome was.

For people who plan and set daily or weekly goals, scheduling time to look at results must be a part of the process. Planners must hold themselves accountable. When results are not acceptable, identify precise steps to improve.

What if, week after week, the planner never seems to get to an actionable part of the plan? If part of the plan is incomplete, prioritize the activities during the review process. In a new plan, remove those parts that no longer have importance. You have to decide whether the action is a priority when not completed after several planning sessions.

Accountability must include self-evaluation when an essential part of the plan is not yet completed after several sessions. When necessary, make personal adjustments. People who are accountable, even though it might not be easy, are far more productive than people who choose not to plan and not to hold themselves responsible.

N — New Directions

Often, new directions emerge with planning. The path of overcoming problems in the plan may require you to go in a new direction. Further courses of action may come along with the planning-accountability phase.

If you're creative, this can be fun. Changing direction shouldn't be seen as a negative.

Like the other actionable parts of planning, it takes time to identify why a new direction will be necessary. During the planning process, use analytical skills and determine why the plan didn't work. What needs to change? There is a difference between giving up and taking a new path to success. The skill of finding solutions benefits those who practice the art of new directions.

Teaching Planning Skills — Keep Things Simple

Planning isn't keeping a schedule or to-do list. Those certainly are a part of getting things done, but they are not the most critical parts of a disciplined planning routine.

Short-term plans include daily and weekly plans. I like to organize my planning process into a weekly format. Long-term planning should also not be overlooked in the process. Learning short-term and long-term planning will provide a young person with lifelong skills.

I experimented over the years with different types of planning tools. I started writing plans and later tried to move to a digital platform. Writing my plan down on paper has been more effective for me. I can keep it in my pocket, where it can be reviewed or modified at any time. I have a friend who uses a journal format. A planning system is a personal choice.

It's crucial to remember that we must find ways to engage youth in the planning process. Keeping things simple will work best. Most youth won't be interested in pursuing a complicated planning method.

Many schools provide students with planning books. When you open the planner, it may have a layout showing one week at a time. This type of planner will be perfect for us as we try to coach our youth and develop planning habits.

Finally, as you teach planning, use my PLAN components. Planning must be a priority, and they must prioritize actionable goals. What is their leadership vision? Is the vision in a weekly plan? Teach them to be accountable and set new directions as appropriate.

Chapter 6

Effectiveness Priority—Time Management

When I facilitate adult leadership workshops, most participants can't wait to learn more about time management. Similarly, as a mentor, you may feel overwhelmed and look forward to learning how to protect your time.

If we don't demonstrate proficiency in managing our time, our mentees will not believe us as we share ideas about time management. Also, time management proficiency provides us with opportunities to give good examples and best practices.

Photography is one of my hobbies. At one point in my life, I considered becoming a professional photographer.

To become skilled at photography, I took classes. My instructors were experts, which accelerated my enthusiasm for artistic opportunities. I was not alone in trusting the teachers. Other students were just as excited about learning from our teachers. We saw their work and listened intently to their stories about successes and failures in the photography business. I was completely comfortable with what I was learning because I knew my teachers were more than teachers; they were practitioners.

As we mentor youth, having practical skills in what we teach is beneficial. You may need to refocus your ability to control your time and accomplish activities that link to your specific goals in the planning process. For the best results as a mentor, you need the self-discipline to teach self-discipline.

Anticipate the Ransacking Raccoon

I had a plan for the day, and I was ready to go. I knew my schedule permitted a lot of focus on my weekly goals, and nothing was going to get in my way. I was going to get things done.

Preparing for the day, I ventured past the sliding glass door leading out to the deck and noticed contemptible chaos. Somebody or something had spewed one of my planters, dirt, and plants over the deck floor and a nearby bench. Upon closer investigation, conspicuous raccoon prints pointed to the ransacker. During the night, a raccoon had climbed onto my deck. Once there, I'm sure the raccoon scavenged for food.

I have had a planter with a few flowering plants sitting on my deck rail for several years. Each year, squirrels visit the plant containers and hide nuts in the soil. The squirrels never disturbed the plants. Because of the gentle hiding of food, I ignored the inconsequential squirrel activity.

The raccoon didn't ignore the opportunity to climb to the deck railing and dig into the planter to find the nuts secured by the squirrels. Not only did the ransacking raccoon decide to dig out the plants, but it also decided to, without care, knock the planter off the deck rail. There was dirt everywhere.

The raccoon's dirty work was not in my plan. It was an interruption. I had to make a decision. Did the cleanup have to happen immediately, or could I wait? Because of the rain forecast and threatening clouds, I chose an immediate cleanup.

Putting my scheduled activities on hold was frustrating, but not performing a cleanup would lead to other problems. With rain and soil mixing, my cleanup would be twice as hard, so I decided to change my plans immediately. Before this minor inconvenience, I had scheduled activities. The raccoon disruption exemplifies how problems can capsize the best intentions.

Anticipate disruptions. Take a moment to identify how many minor inconveniences—acts of ransacking raccoons—have disrupted your day. How did you respond? Would there have been consequences if you had not responded to the disruptions? Are there things you can do to minimize or eliminate the disturbances in the future?

Planning is a life skill that leads to success and accomplishment. To accomplish success, a person has to perform activities associated with the plan. Otherwise, the plan is useless. With that said, effective people anticipate disruptions. They know they must decide whether to act on the disturbances. Some of the actions have to be immediate. Others can take place later.

So what is the best strategy for ransacking raccoon problems? Stay proactive and keep everything in perspective. We must stay calm and positive. It may take some time to clean up the mess of those incoming problems, but you must move forward and refocus.

If not urgent, fix the problem or deal with the interruption later. When taking this approach, you maintain your energy on your primary goals and activities. However, like my rain scenario, you may have to clean up as quickly as possible; otherwise, the problem may get worse.

As a mentor to youth, coach young people to keep a positive attitude. Things could be worse. Can we learn from the experience? Always look for the bright side of a problem.

The raccoon knocked the planter off the deck rail. It fell the right way—the planter fell on my bench. A worst-case scenario might be that I could have been walking under the deck at the time of the incident. A planter full of soil striking me in the head doesn't sound good. Ouch! Focus on reality. Things can always be worse.

After you deal with the problem, get back to the plan. Get your most productive activities done. The most beneficial activities should link to your weekly plan.

What else can we learn from the ransacking raccoon? For one thing, I want to avoid this type of disruption in the future. I might relocate my planter to a lower part of the deck. If the raccoon returns, it will not dislodge the planter from the railing. Take proactive steps to decrease your ransacking raccoon situations.

Even with proactive thinking, I still anticipate a future raccoon visit. No one has complete control of interruptions. Using preventive processes may help decrease them. Stay calm and make decisive decisions about how to deal with challenges. Mentors should point out real-world situations to mentees. Youth can learn strategies to increase effectiveness by overcoming plan-ransackers.

Choose to Block the Ransacking Raccoon

To improve time management, a person should secure time for essential activities and block out frivolous interruptions and disruptions. Interruptions and disruptions are going to happen. However, guarding against ongoing disruptions will significantly improve a person's effectiveness.

Here's a metaphor that may help teach youth to control incessant interruptions. A house will serve as a measure of time in our day, or twenty-four hours. A ransacking raccoon will be an interruption. Finally, in our metaphor, the doorway to our house will be our ability to choose. We all have a choice in how we deal with interruptions.

Imagine the raccoon that visited my home. My neighboring raccoon was outside and did minimal damage to a planter, which interrupted my day because of a cleanup. What would have happened if my door had been open? Allowing a ravenous raccoon to explore my home searching for food is anything but desirable. Damage might not be as bad as letting a bear wander through, but raccoons can be ransacking experts.

It doesn't matter who you are or what you do, there are only twenty-four hours in a day. No matter how much you wish for it, you can't get more hours.

With your house representing twenty-four hours, the door to your home represents a choice. You can choose never to close the door. If you make this choice, anticipate nonstop visits from the outside world. In other words, interruptions will be consistently constant.

Just like the people who choose immediately to deal with every interruption, abandoned buildings with open doors show signs of stress. Nature will take over as all kinds of critters visit and make critter homes inside. The weather will cause internal damage and deteriorate the structure of the building. People wander into the building, and some take what they want or practice art skills on the walls. Mold, dust, and plants will attack ruthlessly. The paint will decay and peel away from the walls.

People who choose to receive every interruption and distraction will eventually feel like a building with an open door. They will burn out mentally and physically.

During workshops focused on leadership and personal effectiveness, some of the adults I worked with communicated that stress from endless interruptions had caused health problems and a feeling of being unbalanced.

Life imbalance can come from not knowing what to do or making no effort to improve time use. What if you choose to play video games during all your free time? Unless you become a professional video game champion, which isn't likely for most people, you'll eventually feel like an abandoned building. Progress and opportunities in life will never come your way.

What is the answer to guarding your most important activities against endless unimportant distractions? Close the door. Choose not to act on distractions, interruptions, and time-wasting activities. Self-awareness is vital in this process.

A person unaware that excessive video gaming will get you nowhere will not close the door. For some, it's easier to withdraw from life and enter a video game fantasy world. Mentors, teachers, and coaches must be willing to provide evidence. A person who chooses to participate in excessive entertainment activities is making a wrong choice.

Mastery of Moments — Using the 90/10 Rule to Optimize Actions and Results

In the military, the Air Force commanders stationed me at Thule Air Force Base in Greenland. Thule, Greenland, is in the Arctic. When I stepped off the plane in August, it was snowing. It was a brutal environment with a beautiful Arctic landscape: icebergs, mountains, snow, punishing wind, freezing temperatures, and more. Greenland is an excellent place to study imbalance.

While in Greenland, I got to observe icebergs up close. The exciting fact about icebergs is that only 10 percent of the iceberg is visible. The remaining 90 percent of the iceberg is under the water. This type of imbalance is observable in nature and beyond the world of nature.

You can use icebergs as a visual to describe imbalance. Draw an iceberg on paper. The waterline should show that 90 percent of the iceberg is below the water. The iceberg will represent actions to achieve a result.

Participants should write the list of highly productive activities into the top 10 percent of the iceberg. The actions are the things that work. They yield the desired results.

In the lower portion of the iceberg, young people can identify activities that do not contribute to the best results. Young people will find the 90/10 situation everywhere in their lives.

Learning Pursuit Pointer #6

Mastery of moments works! If you know the superior actions that will get you exceptional results, choose to do those superior things.

It's important to note that 90/10 is just a general concept. Imbalance can be 95/5, 99/1, or 60/40. The percentage is less important than understanding that a few actions will produce the biggest gains or results. We should all focus on the 10 percent actions.

Most young people I know are very familiar with the music industry. The natural 90/10 imbalance saturates the music industry. There is an imbalance in the number of hit songs in an album release. When artists release a new album, they are thrilled if 10 percent of the songs become hits on the radio or through streaming services.

Look at streaming services and the multitude of musicians. Only 10 percent of the musicians on streaming services earn most of the revenue generated from the services. All musicians want to be in the top 10 percent of earners.

Music festivals are a great way to increase the fan base and make a profit. However, a closer look reveals that most (90 percent) of the audience attend music festivals to see one band. Everywhere you look in the music industry, there is an imbalance.

Clothing might be another area of interest for young people. The clothing industry is full of examples of 90 percent/10 percent. We mostly wear approximately 10 percent to 20 percent of the clothes in our closets. When I first heard of that perspective, I immediately agreed.

How about fashion trends? The fashion industry is excited when the new year's fashion trends arrive. But they know that roughly 10 percent of the fashion trends will dominate 90 percent of people shopping for clothes.

With the two examples I've given you to share with your youth mentee, they should quickly see how the 90/10 imbalance is everywhere. It will help them understand that they may need to look closely at how they use their time. What actions are giving them the best results? Once they identify the 10 percent actions, they will have an opportunity to master moments.

Mastery of moments works! If you know the superior actions that will get you exceptional results, choose to do those superior things.

Chapter 7

Teaching Thinking Skills

It was a beautiful summer day. Our bicycling adventure through the state park trails was a perfect family activity. We thoroughly enjoyed the conversation, exercise, and nature along the winding trails. The trails were full of other bicyclists and hikers. As we passed a waterway, children were playing along the banks. The trail was pristine and well maintained. All of a sudden, a Y intersection provided us with options.

The path to the right followed the winding waterway. It offered more of the same scenery—families, hikers, bicyclists, and a well-maintained bike path. The path to the left led off into a wooded area by way of a dirt trail. We decided to venture down the dirt path, which looked more challenging and offered a different type of scenery.

Not far into our ride on the dirt trail, I noticed old rusted-out barrels, broken down and rotting wood, broken bottles, used beer can clutter, and other garbage scatterings along the sides of the trail. Graffiti covered abandoned structures. On the left side of the trail, there was a high embankment with foliage. Garbage led into the foliage, and I immediately thought the high ground to the left would be a perfect place for someone to hide.

One of my daughters cautiously said, "This looks like a place you would go if you wanted to die." My other daughter agreed. We laughed and turned around.

Make a wise decision. When you find yourself in an area that doesn't feel or look right, it may be best to leave.

How can you avoid finding yourself in an area or situation that might be unsafe? We need to think first and consider systems that help prevent unsafe conditions or any other obstacle.

A system is a group of things or parts that exist and work together. Problem solvers use systems to find the best solutions. Planners like to use systems to ensure positive targeted outcomes.

You can make better decisions when you identify the different parts of a system. Organizations like to look at their systems and create strategic plans. They start by examining each part of the organization. Each unit in the organization should work toward goals that support the vision and mission of the organization.

Drone Perspective to See Systems

To see a system, you have to take a different perspective. While most people might be looking at a problem or opportunity on the ground level, creative thinkers try to get above the opportunity or problem to see the systems.

New technology has allowed firefighters to see from a different perspective. Specifically, drones improve the view of the problem.

Firefighters are known to rush to the scene and gather facts. Sometimes, they climb ladders to observe their challenge visually—identifying the location of the fire, for example. The firefighter on the ladder communicates the location to the command center and fire chief. From the ground, firefighters know that their initial assessment may be wrong.

As leader of the department, the fire chief is always learning about new technologies that help gather specific information at the scene of a fire. A recent advancement in this process is the use of drones. Drones are valuable, as they provide a high perspective above the fire and offer real-time live stream video and thermal imagery of the scene.

Like the modern firefighter, systems thinkers approach things from a different perspective. They focus on a view to see the system because they have system awareness.

Drones with thermal imaging technology allow leaders in the command center to identify precisely where the heat is coming from in a fire. They can also see traffic conditions and the deployment of their firefighters. Based on this information, they quickly adapt to fight the fire.

When thinking critically, we need to see the big picture. In a perspective where systems are not considered—the ground-level view—important information will be missing. We need to elevate to a level of thinking that allows us to see the many connections and how they are interacting. When practicing systems thinking, consider the bigger picture by taking a drone view.

Awareness of the Many Moving Parts

The systems-thinking approach requires an understanding that there is a system, and the system has parts. Critical thinkers have an awareness of systems. They use those systems when thinking about problems or significant opportunities. They want to see and understand all the moving parts.

When using a systems-thinking perspective or teaching systems thinking to your mentee, you should start by identifying the parts of the system. Some people don't think about the intricate nature of a system. Each part of the system has a purpose. Critical thinkers use a systems-thinking strategy to prepare for highly effective results.

To teach this type of thinking, encourage your mentee to identify an upcoming event. What are the systems involved in that event? Brainstorm the smaller parts of the event that will affect the overall outcome or results.

Below is an example of systems-thinking strategies for an event at a local park:

- How will you get there?

- Who is going to drive?

- Who will attend?

- What time should we get there?

- Do we need to leave at a specific time?

- How should we dress?

- What type of shoes should we wear?

- Do we need to bring food and water?

- Who's going to bring mosquito repellent?

- Who's going to bring sunscreen?

- Do we know of any safety issues?

- Are there any dangerous parts of the park?

- Do we have a map of the park?

- Do we need a safety kit in case someone is injured?

- Do we have a plan for situations where someone might get lost?

Systems thinking takes creativity and practice. Problems that appear simple may have hidden complexity. Systems help to identify the moving parts and connections. As you consider and problem-solve with your mentee, look for examples right in front of you.

Resource Awareness

After leaving an unsafe bicycle path, I asked, "How can I avoid finding myself in an area that might be unsafe?" My daughters were with me on the bike ride, which made my question more pressing.

It was the first time we had explored that particular bike trail, but we could have prepared to avoid the problem.

Before engaging in a fun activity—a bicycle ride through an unfamiliar location, for example—research and planning will help to keep you safe. Staying safe is the desired outcome we will utilize as we explore systems.

Before the bicycle ride, a map might have alerted me to a potential problem area outside the official bicycle trail.

Think of times that you found yourself in a bad situation. Did you utilize a map or other resource before the problem? Information is what's needed. Information can serve as a map. Where can you get information that will help you navigate unsafe situations?

Community newspapers or local television news provide information. Before commuting to work, many people watch the news, scan the internet, or listen to a radio broadcast to identify problems. A commuter with knowledge has resources to help make decisions. A commuter can take a different route to avoid delays. Information improves commutes and affects overall safety.

Where are the high-crime areas in a community? Some police departments utilize online crime maps to alert citizens of crime patterns. Online crime maps are another example of an informational resource. People who use informational resources in decision-making have an advantage over those who are unaware or choose not to take advantage of the strategy.

We have an advantage over past generations because of the instant news and other information available through technology.

Even on a bike trail, technology has made getting from point A to point B easier. Everything is online, so it's become simple to research areas and routes using a cell phone.

The right resources, information, and technology help us avoid unsafe situations. However, experiences and wisdom from prior knowledge may lead to a person overriding a technology output. A bicycle trail app on a cell phone might consider an unmaintained trail entirely appropriate. Even with the technology recommendation, my daughters and I could still decide to override the technology based on our own instincts and experiences. Never be afraid to override technology. Technology isn't supposed to rule our lives. Instead, it's a tool to improve our lives. Prior knowledge is essential in our decision-making systems.

Software and apps will not include human intuition, knowledge, skill, life experience, and other personal attributes.

While traveling by car, the fastest route identified by technology might miss details that matter. For example, traveling by city or freeway may not make sense if a person wants to take the scenic route. We can make a choice and override technology.

Trust Your Eyes

After making a decision, evidence collection is still a part of the process and may require a plan change. Dwight D. Eisenhower, the thirty-fourth president of the United States, is given credit for saying, "Plans are worthless, but planning is everything." He was referring to changes needed after activating a plan.

Evidence collection goes hand in hand with decision-making and possible changes to a plan.

The evidence was visible when my daughters and I traveled down the wrong bicycle path. We used what we saw to evaluate and avoid possible unfavorable outcomes. The negative result might have been as simple as getting a flat tire from broken glass. Or, in a worst-case scenario, we might have encountered unfriendly park patrons—bears eating the garbage along the trail. We decided to avoid possible problems.

Part of evidence collection should be observing people. What behaviors do you see? In a park, perhaps the people are carefree and enjoying the scenery as they walk around. People relaxing and enjoying time with family, friends, and nature can send you a message. What if you observe people who don't look at ease and stress-free?

I was once observing a group of youth walking through a city. I was parked, so I had a good view of their behavior. They appeared to be teenagers. They were doing what teenagers do when they get together. It looked like they were enjoying conversation and time together.

Unexpectedly, the youths abruptly stopped. They were all looking intently at something down the street in front of them. I watched them cautiously take a few more steps forward and again stop. Something was making them uneasy. One of the kids turned and ran in the opposite direction of the perceived menace. Immediately, all the other teenagers followed the exiting leader. Their exit behavior was a clear sign to me that there was a possible problem ahead.

I decided not to explore the hidden side of the building. I don't know what startled the kids. However, based on their reactions, I decided not to explore. They didn't look like they needed my help, so I left the area.

Learning and teaching systems thinking can lead to positive results. A systems-think map might have specific information from physical maps, newspapers, community reports, technology resources, and prior knowledge. Depending on the desired results, there may be other informational items needed. After implementation, the person using the systems map can control the process and make changes. A person who knows how to plan by using a systems-think map has a powerful resource but still has the power to choose.

A system is a group of things or parts that exist and work together. Understanding systems requires awareness. Through mentoring, when you share the different parts of a system, you share a thinking skill many people overlook. Understanding systems is valuable to people who think at high levels. And we want our mentees to think at those high levels.

Thinking Pays Off

We must look for ways to help our mentees prepare for the future. We want them to be successful in their current situations and beyond. Some of our mentees will go to college. Other mentees will begin employment. Being college and career ready should be on our minds as we mentor.

As a school administrator, I had the opportunity to facilitate several college-and-career fairs. These were great opportunities to find out what college admission staff and future employers wanted from youth. They came to the events to recruit, but not all students had experiences considered acceptable to recruiters. Not everybody can get into the most popular universities or business settings. Recruiters were looking for young people with potential. I encourage young people to demonstrate potential by sharing past accomplishments and experiences. Recruiters are always looking for youth who can solve problems and think critically. Youth who have experienced academic and extracurricular success likely possess the ability to think at higher levels.

Mentors usually can relate to the qualitative information I gathered from recruiters. As adults, we have all worked with colleagues who seem to be exceptional problem solvers. Since you're reading this book, you're probably a critical thinker. You're looking for better ways to teach youth life skills and self-discipline principles. You're trying to solve a problem or improve. How do you or other critical thinkers solve problems? How did the higher-level thinkers become so productive by thinking differently?

Critical Connections in the Brain

Let's start with a simple perspective of how the human brain works. The brain is a spectacular organ. The world's most powerful computers will never reach a capacity where they can operate like a human brain. Our brains are a miracle!

To explain how to help a mentee with self-control, we don't need to explain all the detailed science associated with how the brain works. However, we should be aware of the importance of our brain and brain health. It is the most crucial organ in our body. Our brain determines our personality. It also operates decision-making, critical thinking, problem-solving, and much more.

Brain research experts are still determining how many cells are in a brain; however, there is some agreement that there are at least fifty billion and one hundred billion neurons (cells). We should not want our neurons to sit idly. Those one hundred billion neurons make approximately ten thousand individual connections with other neurons. Mentors need to facilitate neuron connections.

What makes a person a critical thinker? It isn't the number of neurons in the brain that facilitates critical thinking. Instead, the connections between the neurons make a person more effective at thinking critically.

I believe the ability to think critically is another characteristic of self-control. People who think before they take action demonstrate self-control. Neuron connections are vital in the process. What is the neuron connection? To understand the complex process of a neuron connection, we need more information about a neuron.

Electrical and chemical connections allow our bodies to function. Connections are a way of communication. While the process is super complex, I plan to keep it simple.

Your nervous system is where neuron communication takes place. The nervous system is inside your body. The brain and spinal cord make up the central nervous system. The nervous system receives sensory input through sensors. After the nervous system receives sensory input, the brain takes that information and provides motor output. The central nervous system is the control center of our body. Neurons are the primary cell in the nervous system. There are different types of neurons, but most neurons have some common features.

Neurons are a transmitting mechanism in the nervous system. Neurons are communication devices. Neurons have three primary function areas:

- Soma—the cell body

- Dendrites—the part of the cell that receives a signal (inbound)

- Axon—generally more extended than dendrites, this part of the cell sends a signal (outbound)

Through chemical or electrical signals, axons connect to dendrites, muscles, or other tissue. The axon communicates with the other organ, telling the cell what to do. At the end of the axon are axon terminals. The neuron communication takes place at the axon terminal.

A synapse is a microscopic gap at the end of the axon terminal. Neurons or other target tissue share information at the synapse.

Impulses on the axon travel more efficiently because of insulating cells around the axon. The insulating cells are called the myelin sheath. Many myelin sheaths can insulate the axon. The gap between the myelin sheath is called the node of Ranvier, and the gap helps in the communication process by increasing the conductivity of nerve impulses.

A neuron transmits electrical signals called nerve impulses. After the nerve impulse, the neuron releases a chemical to a nearby neuron over the synapse gap.

With experiences, new memories, or learning, there is a change in the nervous system. Scientists call the change neuroplasticity: changes in synapses and other parts of neurons.

For physical or mental learning, neuron pathways must form or strengthen. Strengthening or creating pathways can be synaptic or structural. Synaptic means that over time given many impulses, the targeted dendrite response increases. Structural strengthening or creating refers to increasing physical connections (sprouting) between the axon and dendrite. Scientists call the response increase potentiation.

Scientists have also identified the opposite of potentiation. A weak response between neurons is called depression. When referring to the term depression with regard to neuron pathways, scientists are not talking about the psychological definition of depression. When there is no strengthening or creation of neuron pathways over time, the synaptic and structural situations look much different from potentiation. In depression, the response from the receiving neuron communication is low or stops. The dendrite target receives fewer impulses. Structurally, the neuron begins pruning connections.

A professional violinist makes everything look easy—neuron pathways have been created and strengthened. Movements happen instantly and so quickly that an observer visually can't keep up and comprehend what is happening.

The musician reads music and simultaneously produces the exact sound on the violin. The physical movements of arms, hands, and fingers flow like water. The professional violinist brings forth a quality of sound that comes from precision positioning of the body. You can almost feel the emotion coming from the musician to the observers.

A fan with no music background might ask whether a professional violinist is a great musician because of muscle memory. Did they memorize the movements? Muscle memory isn't the answer. Instead, it's a brain functioning at a high level. The brain controls all the physical actions through neurological pathways. For the professional violinist, the pathways are refined and strengthened in the brain.

Professional Pathways

The brain needs to work repetitively to strengthen neuron pathways. A professional violinist worked their brain for years. The work is called practice. Through practice, the brain pathways secure and refine.

My brain has no brain pathways developed to play the violin. To play the violin, even at a beginner level, I would have to change the structure of my brain. It would take time to develop pathways. Over time, if I practiced enough, I might play simple music on the violin, but it would take a lot of time and work.

What would happen if we asked a professional violinist with no experience in car repair to fix a car? That extremely talented individual might find fixing a car's electrical problem challenging, if not impossible. If the violinist had no experience as a vehicle mechanic, would the violinist troubleshoot the problem? Could the violinist find the circuit board causing the electrical system failure? Would the violinist know the tools needed to diagnose or fix the problem? They would not have the brain pathways developed like an experienced technical mechanic. A certified technical mechanic has the brain pathways developed because of experiences dealing with similar problems and education, so mechanics enjoy the troubleshooting process. However, they will not be ready to perform in a music concert.

Although the two professions are different, the mechanic and the violinist might have similar abilities at problem-solving and higher-level thinking. Although the structural layout of their brains might be completely different, both might have neurological pathways that have been created and strengthened for problem-solving.

Our goal should be to provide opportunities for our mentees to be experts at higher-level thinking. We do this by providing them with learning opportunities and experiences. We can teach them how to think more effectively and thereby change their brains by strengthening and creating neuron pathways. Higher-level thinking facilitates self-control.

Problem-Solving

Now that we have fundamentals about how the brain works, we have an opportunity to help our mentees think. It's exciting that we can teach, model, and explain thinking skills to our mentees, propelling them through life. Preparing them to be problem solvers, critical thinkers, and possess the ability to think at higher levels should be a mentor's responsibility.

Learning Pursuit Pointer #7

If you want to stand out from the crowd, you should become a problem solver. Highly effective problem solvers take proactive steps to improve this life skill.

Most teachers have learned about how to teach at higher levels. They prepare lessons with specific questions and objectives for their students. Their goal is to use high-quality instruction to help youth learn and to provide challenging opportunities that facilitate higher levels of thinking.

Working with teachers, I know how important it is to teach at higher levels. My goal as an administrator was to provide the opportunities, guidance, and coaching to help teachers teach beyond simple thinking and memorization techniques so their students were challenged to think critically.

I like the idea of mentors using teacher skills. We need to teach mentees how to problem-solve. They should know how to overcome challenges and produce positive results. Their problem-solving skills will benefit them throughout life. They will only sometimes have teachers, coaches, and mentors guiding them. We need to provide the experiences. With skills, they will be much more prepared for college and career-ready situations. We should all want to rewire brains so the person with the rewired brain can think for themselves. Exceptional results consistently come from people who are problem solvers.

The professional violinist and expert car technician might have vital problem-solving neuron pathways. Experiences or thinking strategies might have affected more than their profession. Like most problem solvers, they have developed thinking skills. Help produce young problem solvers by engaging them with the following:

- High-quality questions

- Organizational strategies

- Fact-finding sessions

- Real-world applications

- Think-first approaches

- Systems thinking

- Breathing strategies

Chapter 8

Mentor-Led Goals

For seven years, I facilitated an aspiring principal program. I allowed the assistant principal participants to develop project-based activities during the program. I found that the assistant principals learn much from planning and initiating projects to help students. Teams were often involved, so they benefited from leadership experiences and creating and following through on a project.

The life of an assistant principal is chaotic and very time intensive. They don't always control their time, but they need to manage the time they do control. Most of the assistant principals were able to achieve their goals. I felt strongly that the experiences would help them in the future.

Learning Pursuit Pointer #8

Mentors should design experiences for mentees. Your mentee can learn from experiences.

Unfortunately, a few assistant principals didn't prioritize the learning projects. They never were able to benefit from the experience. Even with my guidance, they could not succeed in the project development activity. I understood how chaotic and time-consuming their positions were, but all the assistant principals had to deal with this problem. Perhaps I could have set more precise expectations. Expectations are a critical part of project development in a mentorship.

With expectations, the mentor and the mentee will have a blueprint or plan for the learning process. I highly recommend that you set expectations if you utilize projects.

Write the Expectations

How should we write the expectations? Keep things simple with our mentees. For example, in working with the assistant principals, I could have increased our project completion success rate.

First, the expectation should include what the mentee will do and what I will do. The unsuccessful assistant principals might have had much more success completing a project if I had communicated more clearly that I would be there to assist.

In addition to direct assistance, I could have made it an option to have scheduled private meetings to review project progress. The meetings might have helped me identify problems and provide help through interventions.

Some of the assistant principals were overwhelmed with their school responsibilities. I believe that is the primary reason most didn't complete the project. By meeting and reviewing their daily schedules, I could have provided recommendations.

What must the mentee do? Although it was a volunteer-type situation, all participants truly wanted to improve their chances and opportunities to become principals. My recommendations were necessary. I observed many paths to a principal position. I observed skills desired by committees, parents, boards of education, and superintendents through the hiring process. For this reason, the assistant principals needed to follow through on developing timelines, plans, implementation actions, and assessments to see if the project made a difference in student academic achievement.

Don't forget that the written expectations should include input from both the mentor and mentee.

Just as the mentor must listen and focus on goals set by the mentee, the mentee must follow through on their action plan. They must participate and take action in the learning process. I did hear some say, "I'm too busy." The excuses may have been factual. Unfortunately, I heard from their statement that they didn't have the follow-through skills needed. If they decided not to follow through on the projects, they missed the learning experience. They were making a choice.

My responsibility as a mentor was to point out the importance of committing to learning and action. Although I would provide feedback on the progress of their goal, they had to choose whether or not they would complete the experiences.

Mentors have an essential role in helping mentees find ways to experience learning. Mentors must ask specific questions about why a mentee is unsuccessful with experiences and then become expert listeners to help set goals and expectations.

Measure Progress

Because I go a little overboard on physical fitness activities, I have had the opportunity to break my body down to where I need assistance. Physical therapists have jumped in to help me regain my physical fitness goals.

Physical therapists use goal setting and measurement to help their clients. As a client, I've had the chance to watch how physical therapists address specific needs and measure progress. As mentors, we can learn from their process.

All of my adventures with physical therapy have started with an interview. During an interview, the therapist seeks to understand the client's past fitness levels and discuss future goals. Physical therapists are generally good listeners.

In addition to getting to know the client, the physical therapist should be aware of facts. They like to use the information before starting a physical therapy regimen of strengthening and stretching.

Clients share specifics about problems. In my case, knee surgeries and arthritis were facts in my life. X-rays, MRIs, and other reports from doctors help physical therapists do their job. This type of information provides a greater understanding of the physical problems.

A mentor can use the same type of process. What do we know about the mentee? How can we help them?

We can start by collecting information about their school grades. Do we see any challenges? Parents should be able to provide us with grades. Grades are facts.

Parents, coaches, and friends might be able to provide us with additional information. I have had parents share information about academic performance and student disabilities. This helped me as I planned activities to meet my mentee's learning styles.

Knowing about disabilities will help us as we mentor, providing the mentor a better perspective on ways to help.

Try to think of other measurements and data that could be helpful: goals, types of academic classes, maturity level, hobbies, interests, and more. This information will help as we look for opportunities to measure success. Again, just as we did for the expectations, we must write down what we plan to measure.

Because most of my current mentees are young, I discuss and write down goals with the parents. I always adjust and fine-tune my plans as I learn additional information from working with the youth.

Check for Improvement

Following writing expectations and measuring progress, mentors should use an assessment to check for improvement. Again, put it in writing. Everything needs to be written down.

My physical therapist identified when we would measure progress. An example of physical therapy measurement might be flexibility measurements of the leg. With arthritis, I had limited flexibility; but after working with the physical therapist over a period of time, I improved my flexibility. The initial measurement served as a baseline.

If you've undergone physical therapy, you know that stretching and strengthening include pain. For mentors and our mentees, it will likely not be so painful. We need to move forward with our plan. Rather than pain, it will be rewarding to see your mentee improve. Checking for improvement shows proof of progress.

Mentee Passionate Engagement

When you're developing mentor-led goals, it's essential to remember that this is an opportunity to engage your mentee. They can add actionable items that you may never have thought of.

I was once mentoring a young person who struggled with self-discipline. He was always getting in trouble at school. I tried to change his direction in life by mentoring him.

I met with him and his parent and developed mentoring expectations. During the meeting, he shared that he had observed me taking photos at sporting events. He wanted to learn photography, so we wrote it in the plan.

I never would have thought to add photography when developing expectations, but my mentee's input made a difference. He was excited about learning to take photos, and that led to improvements at school.

We scheduled times when we could go to sporting events and take photos. I taught him how to use the equipment, and he became proficient at sports photography.

Checking his discipline records became enjoyable for me because I saw him improving. He became engaged in the expectations because he had had the opportunity to participate in writing our goals.

Writing a mentor-led goal might sound a little boring to a young person. Find a way to engage the young person by including actions or activities they're passionate about. Like my mentee who became more engaged in school because of photography, you might have a young person who will benefit from adding a specific action to the mentor-led goals. Mentee participation will improve mentoring outcomes.

Chapter 9

8 Aspects of Communication

Have you ever been interrupted while talking to someone? Did you think they were listening? People who interrupt appear uninterested in your ideas. This can be frustrating and provide problems for the relationship.

As we try to build relationships with our mentees, we must be good listeners. Since listening skills are so critical, we need to not only model listening skills but also teach listening skills.

Mentors must participate in a balancing act: share information and listen closely to the mentee. Interrupting people can lead to a chip in the framework of the relationship, which is exactly what we don't want.

Interruptions can also lead to a break in the relationship that will be hard to repair. Your mentee may not want to be involved in the mentorship because of your constant inability to listen.

I have had vast experience working with teachers. One of my goals was to mentor them and make them better teachers. After observations in the classroom, I was usually enthusiastic to provide feedback and share what I observed so the teacher could improve. Teacher improvement means improved student academic achievement.

Conferences after an observation were usually short, without much time to share ideas. Sometimes I would catch myself moving too quickly and pressing my point of view. While my information was important, I had to make an effort to slow down and focus on listening, allowing the teacher to share and ask questions.

I could tell by the person's reaction when I was going too fast or pressing my ideas. I learned to observe facial expressions. The next time you interrupt a person, watch their face. Do they look happy that you just interrupted them?

If you're preparing to talk while someone else is talking, you're not listening with focus. A better strategy is just to listen. When you try to prepare a response instead of listening, you miss an opportunity to understand. I believe most people are aware when a person isn't listening. That can be harmful to any relationship.

We must be cautious as mentors not to neglect the listening process. Most mentors have more experience than the mentees. Most mentors probably have a good answer to problems. Based on experience, many mentors rush to share ideas and points of view. You would think this would be a positive. However, mentees don't see it that way. They may simply feel that their mentor isn't listening to them.

Focus Like the Board Breaker

I have coached and mentored as a martial arts instructor. As soon as I tell people that I'm a martial arts instructor, many bring up board breaking. Our school isn't much into breaking boards, but we sometimes use board breaking to teach focus and technique. I understand that board breaking is a significant visual in most people's heads when they think of martial arts, so I appreciate that the people bringing it up are trying to make some connection to our activities.

Let's compare board breaking skills and listening skills. Imagine the intense face of a martial artist staring at a stack of boards. You can tell by their intensity and focus that the karate grand master (karate expert) is ready to scream as soon as they strike.

One thing I've noticed about students breaking boards is that their focus is on the board. Whether they are successful at breaking the board or not, they focus on the board. Imagine if our listening skills were that focused.

Be aware of your situation. When talking with another person, put energy and effort into what you're doing. Highly effective communicators are aware of their actions and the actions of the person with whom they are speaking. The ability to focus is a high-level communication skill.

Make Eye Contact

To break boards in martial arts, you must first focus on the target. The board breaker's eyes never wander around the training facility or at others observing. Even when I speak and coach during breaking, others rarely look at me. The focus is always on the board.

When listening to others, do your eyes wander or look at the person speaking? It's an excellent strategy to have good eye contact as we coach. Eye contact tells the speaker we're listening. Good listeners should use their eyes but not stare.

As we teach listening skills, remember that the eye contact strategy might include cultural differences. My Korean martial arts teacher shared with students that making eye contact could be considered aggressive or disrespectful. However, some youth with no negative cultural component may not know the benefits. We need to teach them this communication skill.

Don't Multitask

Are there similarities between what a skilled and intense karate board breaker looks like and an expert listener? The listener also shows intent. They demonstrate that they want to hear the speaker's point of view. They intentionally stop doing other things and listen. The karate board breaker doesn't multitask while challenged with a stack of boards.

How do you feel when you have a conversation with someone who appears not to be listening? Bosses send powerful messages to employees if they listen well or not. Mentors can learn from negative experiences with supervisors who don't seem to be listening—communication strategies not to use while with your mentee.

Imagine the supervisor who makes almost no eye contact. During your meeting, he types a message on his cell phone and constantly looks down at his phone for messages or to check the time. Because of past behavior, you know that if a call comes in, he'll take it. This boss seems fixated on technology rather than listening. Some mentors and parents also have this problem while with youth.

I was once responsible for monitoring alarms and alerts that could come in through my electronic devices. When meeting with employees, I shared information about the emergency alerts—if I get a message, I may have to check to see if the message is an emergency alert. When I received a signal on my cell phone, I would apologize for the interruption and quickly check the phone. I immediately put the phone away if it was not an emergency alert.

If you're around young people, teach them the importance of focus. For example, you might ensure they put their phones down during meals. You may even have to remove the phone from their hands and put the device somewhere else. Make this a routine as you also model communication skills.

If you catch yourself being an ineffective listener, do something about it. Consider making some changes and make it a goal to improve. Write the goal down. You will send a message: I care what you have to say. As mentors, we are the role models. We must have a significant focus as listeners, just like a leader with highly effective listening skills.

Check Your Power

Have you ever had a supervisor who practiced poor speaking and listening skills? It can be frustrating. You may have found that there always seemed to be a communication breakdown and power imbalance.

In the eyes of most people, a supervisor has power. Their power comes from some designated employee structure that has them in a leadership position. Some of our bosses may have been physically powerful as well. For fun, think of your boss as having the power to break a stack of one-inch-thick pine boards.

I have seen physically strong people come into a martial arts training facility. Many of these lacked technical skills, but they were powerful. What do you think happened when they had to break boards? You probably guessed they could use power to smash through the boards. Even with a lack of technique, board breaking was not a problem. However, they may never reach their potential if they don't focus on skills and techniques. The power through actions will only take them so far. This is the same when someone in a power position (leader, supervisor, coach, or mentor) communicates from a power position. We all need to work on our communication skills.

I've also observed leaders who powered through conversations. They appeared neither interested in listening nor open to ideas. They considered their way to be the only way, and they were quick to share their point of view with little interest in other perspectives.

General George Patton, one of America's most famous military commanders, was successful and known for powering through communications. He gave orders and expected people to follow those orders. His communication methods helped American allies liberate Europe from the Nazis. He is a fascinating leader; however, most leaders can't succeed with Patton-like communication skills.

Powering through communication techniques worked well for General Patton during wartime, but it may not help build respect and trust if you're trying to build a relationship. We must be careful not to cut off the thoughts of others. Sometimes mentors and leaders accidentally do this.

Engage Conversations

What are some ways to engage your mentee in conversations? Engagement might be as simple as asking questions or listening with empathy.

When you ask your mentee a question, you send a message that you want to learn more, and you're showing an interest in their ideas. The results of the questioning could increase your understanding. We should all want to find out more about our mentees. Asking questions helps us do this.

Being empathetic is a way to tell your mentee that you understand their perspective. When you demonstrate empathy during communication, you can verbally reflect what you believe to be the feelings of your mentee. The following comments are an example of showing empathy:

- I can see how that must have been stressful.

- I can tell that you don't feel good about the situation.

- I can see how you must feel like a total success.

- I can only imagine how good it must have felt getting an A after studying for hours.

- That must have been exhausting.

If you try to practice empathy during conversations, you should be sincere. This isn't a communication trick. People can ascertain when someone is trying to be manipulative. Reflecting with empathetic responses is an effective way to build better relationships. Again, we should never use communication tricks to try to fake our way through a conversation.

Dial In Your Speed

Effective communication skills also require a little more time than some are willing or able to provide.

I was on the second floor when the call came in. An assistant principal called for help on the radio, "We need help in the cafeteria!"

The cafeteria was in the basement area. I started jogging to the nearest stairwell from the second floor. "I'm on the way," I broadcasted clearly on the radio. I thought he sounded like it was an emergency as I moved through the hallway.

After reaching the second-floor stairwell door, a teacher stepped out of his door across from the stairwell entrance.

"I need to talk to you about Johnny! Do you have a minute?" The teacher looked upset.

While trying to look calm, I stated, "I have a situation downstairs. I can't talk now, but I'll be back."

Although I didn't get a chance to take in all aspects of his facial expression, I could tell that my response made him frustrated. He made eye contact, glared directly into my eyes, and spoke quickly, "This is important!"

I turned slightly in his direction, "I have an emergency downstairs. Can I come back?"

He started walking back into his room and said, "Sure!"

I went down the stairs and helped the assistant principal in the cafeteria. After solving the problem in the cafeteria, I went back to the teacher on the second floor. The Johnny situation was not an emergency, but my short conversation annoyed the teacher.

Although my example is an extreme case of quick communication, speeding through communication can sometimes be ineffective.

Those who speed through the communication process might feel that they're accomplishing their goal. They might leave a meeting and think they successfully communicated ideas. But they leave many people wondering, *What in the world did that person just say?* There will be others who don't care what was just said. No change or action will take place because of the communication problem.

There are times you need to get the message out quickly, such as during emergencies. I'm sure General Patton didn't have time to sit on a committee and listen empathetically to all committee members. He had to make decisions. I didn't have time to discuss the Johnny situation immediately with the teacher; I had to go to another part of the building.

I have observed board breakers utilize speed. Speed helps some martial artists smash through boards. However, like the mighty breakers with no technique, their speed only got them so far. They still needed technique and skill to be the best they could be.

During the communication process, we need to dial, or pay attention to, the speed with which we communicate. It's important to be aware of time and to build in a reasonable amount of time for listening.

Develop the Right Timing

Let's consider one more connection between board breaking and communication. Timing is critical to the success of both.

Six one-inch-thick boards were placed back-to-back on concrete blocks, ready for me to break. Six inches of wood is a challenge. When I hovered over the boards, my instructor commented, "You will need a lot of technique." I agreed. A sledgehammer might easily smash through the boards, but striking it with the palm of your hand is a different story. People who routinely smash through an obstacle like that have special techniques and skills.

As in most sports, physics and science are essential to success. Athletes focus on the fundamentals. One physical element that will help the breaker is turning the hips into the strike. Rotating the hips increases the force on impact because of weight distribution.

You can coach people on how to turn their hips, but if their timing is off, they probably won't succeed. If you turn your hips too soon or too late, the boards may not splinter. Failing to break the boards will also hurt physically. Hard objects are an obstacle to the hands.

Just like breaking boards, the skill of listening requires timing. If you try to force your ideas quickly, you may find people become suspect and wonder what you're selling.

I met many angry people while working in a school. They would storm into my office with some problem, often bypassing teachers and assistant principals to get to me. When they arrived, they were clearly upset about their situation.

I learned it was ineffective to share information immediately with angry people. They were emotional and often didn't have all the facts. If I tried to provide them with facts upfront, I was in for a challenge. They didn't want to hear anything I had to say. Instead, they wanted me to listen to their information. The timing was critical.

Just because they were emotional didn't mean that I had to agree with them. I learned the importance of timing my response but not showing agreement with information that was not true. For example, unless you agree, you should not move your head up and down as you listen. That action generally signals agreement. That perception of agreement might create further problems when you share your different perspectives.

Angry communicators will sometimes ask questions. When that occurs, your green light, your communication opportunity, is on. You can provide facts about the situation. Answering their questions doesn't interfere with someone who is venting.

Slight delays in venting can also provide an opportunity. The time might be right to ask clarifying questions such as "Where did you get that information?" Probing for information at the right time is an effective way to show interest and gather the information you need to make decisions.

It's also important to ask questions or probe for information in a respectful voice, presenting with confidence. To become confident as a communicator, you must practice your skills. Not everyone immediately becomes a confident presenter. However, angry or forceful people will interpret your presentation as weak if you don't focus on this skill.

Probing questions might look like the following:

- Where did you get this information?

- Where does that happen?

- When did this happen?

- Who was there?

- How do you know?

- Can you give me a little bit more detail?

Asking probing questions and asking for clarification at the right time can show the speaker that you're interested in learning more. Again, it's essential to ask questions at the appropriate time.

Observe the listener as you probe for information and ask specific questions. What does their body language tell you? Perhaps they are so stressed out that asking a probing question might be taken as you trying to take over the conversation. Observe the person closely to identify when it's appropriate to ask questions.

Emotional mirroring is a part of the communication process. If you look like you don't care, you can almost guarantee a communication breakdown. If they're already angry, their anger will increase. The conversation could get out of control if you meet aggression with aggression. I'm pretty tolerant and will listen to an aggressive person. However, I have my limits. If a person is too aggressive, I will end the conversation.

Hapkido is a martial arts style that involves avoiding an attack. If someone throws a punch in your direction, getting out of the way is the number one priority. You can get out of the way by turning or sliding to the side. Meeting the attack straight on is a collision the hapkido practitioner tries to avoid.

In our effort to become highly effective communicators, the hapkido technique may be helpful when a person is aggressive. Don't meet aggression with aggression. Instead, stay calm and confident. Don't take aggressive behavior personally. Be aware that the person you're listening to is emotional and may need time to vent. This will allow you to look for the appropriate time to ask questions and probe.

The timing of knowing when to share specific facts and your perspective comes with the experience of working with others. We must share important information. Communication isn't a one-way activity. Immediately pressing my information into the conversation will not work with angry people. However, after the person vents and you find out their perspective, you need to share your perspective or provide facts.

How does all this communication information apply to working with a mentee? I have yet to find a young person who doesn't run into emotional situations with peers or siblings. These perceived or actual communication conflicts are perfect times for a mentor to teach. Ask the mentee how they handled the communication problem. Share with them ideas about how to improve their communication skills. If they were emotional and became aggressive toward the other person, share the benefits of getting out of the way (hapkido) and timing their responses.

I've told many young people that they should consider every conflict with another person a learning experience. We learn by dealing with difficult situations. We miss an opportunity if we never know how to communicate, deal with the challenges, and learn communication timing skills.

Have Confidence

We know the timing in the communication process is very important. Sharing too soon or too late might be a mistake—communication may break down. None of us are perfect at communication. It takes practice, and we get better through experience. With experience, hopefully, our mentees will become more confident communicators.

> **Learning Pursuit Pointer #9**
> *People gain confidence in their abilities by preparing in advance and having experience in the communication process.*

While being transported to basic training at Lackland Air Force Base in Texas, I observed a bus driver communicate confidently. All the young people on the bus were listening attentively.

The bus came to an unexpected stop just outside the gates. Everyone on the bus was sitting quietly, and only the bus driver seemed at ease. Although the passengers were young, you could see the stress in their eyes.

The timing of the bus stop was curious to me. I wasn't sure what to expect. The driver stood from his seat and faced the back of the bus. He didn't have to request attention—every young person looking at him was listening intently. He scanned the audience, which seemed to add stress to the circumstances.

The bus driver paused and then looked confidently throughout the bus. He stood tall, appeared to be making eye contact with each person on the bus, and pointed to the gates. "You're about to have a change in life.

When you go through those gates, everything will change." His speech was not long or detailed. But I remember it as if it was yesterday. His final comment was about believing in yourself and doing what you must to succeed through the upcoming training. It was up to us to succeed in the upcoming challenge.

When he finished, the young people on the bus didn't ask any questions or comment to other passengers. No one cheered. No one said thank you for the advice. But I bet every person on that bus remembers the timing and confidence of the presenter. Interestingly, although he didn't know a single person on the bus, he seemed to care about us enough to share some words of wisdom. He wanted to pass along a message. Looking back, I should have thanked the driver for his encouraging comments.

After his perfectly timed and confident presentation, the driver returned to his seat, and the bus moved toward the gates.

I have no idea if the driver provided us with his words of wisdom officially or if it was spontaneous. He was not in military uniform. I know one thing; he said it with confidence. He was right that my life was going to change. I needed to stay focused on upcoming training goals to become a successful airman in the United States Air Force.

Confidence during the communication process makes a difference. People will notice if you don't have confidence when you speak.

After coming through those gates at Lackland Air Force Base, I read a message posted inside the base: "Whether you think you can, or you think you can't—you're right." That famous quote is attributed to Henry Ford, founder of Ford Motor Company. I had a chance to think about the message daily in basic training. We can apply and teach our mentees this message as we work on their communication skills.

People gain confidence in their abilities by preparing in advance and having experience in the communication process. The best communicators are sincere and confident.

Chapter 10

Facts and Focus in Conversation

As a principal, I had to investigate many incidents: crimes, he-said-she-said problems, assaults, offensive touching, and more. For example, if the fire alarm signaled, it was time to act first and then investigate. When a student entered the office crying and shared a problem through the weeping, I had to sort through emotions to find facts. Investigation was part of the job, but fact-finding can be helpful in day-to-day communications.

Not all mentoring situations require fact-finding. But some mentors might work with very challenging young people. Here are a few strategies that worked for me.

I mentored Dwayne and observed his interactions with others. He had what it takes to become a leader, but his immaturity and following-the-crowd habits were holding him back.

Dwayne and I met often for problems and to celebrate his improvement efforts. Among his problems were disrupting class, cutting class, vandalism, poor academic efforts, lying, and bullying others.

Dwayne's grandmother and I stayed in touch about his progress and problems. She wanted him to succeed but didn't always believe that he was in the wrong. Note-taking was extremely important in this mentoring situation because I wanted to identify what happened. This way, the grandmother and I could partner to help him improve. For example, when he broke into a car in the parking lot, I interviewed him and took detailed notes. I also took notes as I interviewed witnesses. Note-taking helped Dwayne and his grandmother see what had happened. We built our partnership to help Dwayne by sharing facts.

During the interview process with Dwayne, I would ask questions. In addition to my trying to find out what happened, he didn't seem to understand why he was in the wrong. Questions helped me gather facts and allowed him to see deeper into his thought process at the time he was making a mistake. Before questioning, he was defensive and said, "I didn't do it!" We found out through the questioning that he liked to show off when he was with his peers, which often got him in trouble. Unfortunately, he *did* do it.

Through the questioning process, it was hard to follow the story. Dwayne was highly emotional. He would jump from one part of the story to another. It's essential when you're working with a mentee like Dwayne that you help focus the conversation. I knew that the only way I could help this young person was to help him understand what was happening when he was following the group. If I could get this to happen, he could make better decisions and walk away.

After note-taking and asking questions, I would sort through the facts. I had to remember the objective: help Dwayne live up to his potential by identifying the problem and solutions to change the poor behavior. My notes were sometimes chaotic, and it was a challenge to find information that would help Dwayne learn from his mistakes.

After a few years of mentoring, Dwayne earned his way to join the school leadership team. During that time, his behavioral problems disappeared, and his grades improved. It took much time and documentation to help him understand his potential, but it was worth it. As a student leader, he would go out of his way to help others and was on his way to a successful school experience.

If you're mentoring a young person like Dwayne, you can use strategies like note-taking, asking questions, maintaining focus, and sorting facts. Also, teach young people the fact-finding and focus process because those skills can be helpful to young and old.

Take Notes

If you try fact-finding too soon, an emotional person might not appreciate your interruption. Timing is essential with this communication skill.

When interviewing students, I had to assure them I would help them through the storytelling process. I needed details to help them identify what had happened. For every situation, there was a story. Stories can be complicated, so I often took notes. Note-taking can help organize the sequence of events, and youth will sometimes tell stories out of sequence.

For those who like to take notes with technology devices, you might want to first let the speaker know what you're doing so they're clear on why you're using your device.

Ask Questions

Asking questions can enhance fact-finding. It tells the person that you're trying to understand their perspective. I wanted to hear what students had to say, and questions supported this effort. My questions were not of a high-level or critical-thinking nature. Instead, they were questions that were logical and based on facts. I used fundamental questions to gather information. For example, basic questions looked like the questions below:

- Were you in the classroom when you heard her say that?

- Were you sitting close to the person to hear what was said?

- How far away were you from the fight?

- What did you see?

- Were there other witnesses?

- What was said?

- What did you say?

- What was the sequence of events?

- What did you do when this occurred?

- How did the person react?

Questioning helps the person who is sharing information. My questions would take them back to the event or what they observed. After considering my questions, students often analyzed what they heard and saw. Questioning helped them sort through the many details to evaluate their actions and the actions of others.

Fact-finding was a contributing communication component. I recommend not using scripted or formulated questions. Let the questions emerge from the dialogue between you and the other person. A question checklist might be too rigid. Let your questions come from the heart and exploration.

The questions should be sincere. We want to become experts at listening, not interrogating. If you listen first and introduce fact-finding questions, you will hopefully improve the clarity of the communication.

The workday for most assistant principals is usually pretty crazy. They move fast to survive the surge of problems and duties. Because of this, these leaders sometimes hurry investigations. I was guilty of that at times, an assistant principal who sometimes aimed to be efficient rather than effective. Unfortunately, striving first for efficiency led to further problems: students didn't feel heard; parents were upset that their child couldn't tell their side of the story; the assistant principal missed essential information in the investigation because they rushed through a conversation; the principal became a part of the process because parents were upset.

You might have an extremely challenging life that requires quick decisions and action. You have to move quickly. Quick interactions, however, might not truly make us more effective.

Efficiency doesn't equal effectiveness. If we communicate verbally or with our body language that we don't have enough time to listen, the listener can perceive that we don't care. As mentors, we need to lead by example.

Overwhelmingly, whenever I tried to hurry through the communication process, I caused myself additional work. There was also a chance that my neglect of fact-finding, focus, and consideration of the other person's feelings could damage the relationship.

I encourage you to self-evaluate your listening process. Your mentee is observing you. You may have to slow down the pace of communication to avoid impending problems.

Maintain Focus

I make it a priority to focus on better listening techniques. Focus can be a problem for a young mentee, so you may need to help them if they drift from one topic to another, politely pointing out the reason for the refocus so they see the value of your suggestion.

Have you ever taken a photograph and the primary subject is out of focus? Before autofocus cameras, amateur photographers often found their pictures out of focus. To bring the primary subject into focus, the photographer manipulated the camera lens. When you pick up a camera with a lens that requires manual focus, you need to adjust the lens. The adjustment might require rotating the cylinder of the lens clockwise or counterclockwise.

In portraiture, the photographer usually focuses on the model's eyes because the eyes of the subject must always be in focus. Like the photographer, we need skills to bring a conversation back to focus.

Learning Pursuit Pointer #10

The fact-finding and focus process isn't a trick or tactic to get your way.
Instead, it's a method to improve the communication process.

Have you ever had a conversation with someone who continually changes the topic, switching from one subject to another? Emotional people might do this often, which causes challenges for the listener.

Good listeners find ways to guide the conversation back to the primary topic. To do this, be observant of what is happening and remain courteous to the speaker. If we fail to take a proactive approach in the conversation, the speaker may continue to jump from topic to topic.

Ask probing questions to regain focus on the primary topic. Share that you need more information because of the discussion complexity. It would help if you tried to guide the conversation with questions about the facts that seem to be most important to the conversation.

The fact-finding and focus process isn't a trick or tactic to get your way. Instead, it's a method to improve the communication process. The goal is to be a good listener and teach our mentees these listening skills.

Sort Facts

Let's use the example of manually focusing a camera lens as a metaphor to identify your objective.

Your mentee loves sport. She plays in a field hockey game and has invited you to the event. You promised to take some photographs of the game. You borrowed a camera from a friend and found that the camera has a manual focus. This is going to be a challenge.

At the event, you have one objective: to take photographs of your mentee playing in the fast-moving game. You find out quickly that a manual focus lens requires special skills because the athletes rush in and out of focus.

To complicate matters, you see a problem with the background of your scene. In the viewfinder, the scene has distracting secondary subjects, which can ruin a photograph. Challenges include the following:

- Porta-potties

- Trash cans

- Trees that seem to grow out of your subject's head

- Overenthusiastic fans jumping into the scene

Listening can be like the challenge a photographer sees at a sporting event. Focusing is fundamental to success. Experienced and skilled sports photographers are aware of what they can control. They can move to avoid secondary subject problems. For example, they may get the porta-potty out of the background by moving ten yards down the sideline. They also plan ahead so they know where the action will take place and can focus on that area.

For the listener, following the action means sorting through facts to reach understanding. Background information might be necessary. We can gain that information by listening closely, organizing our thoughts, and asking appropriate questions.

As we listen, we must be like the sports photographer. We can identify those crucial ideas and fundamental components that help us focus. We must also keep the sequence of events organized. At times, the person communicating might accidentally leave out essential story parts. Missing information can be as disruptive to the content as other distractions. Speaking and listening take practice.

Role-Play Communicate

As we work with our mentees, they might benefit from activities to practice listening and speaking. We can take a proactive approach and teach the skills through role-playing.

While role-playing, young people can learn concepts more thoroughly than other teaching methods. During role-playing activities, we can coach and provide support. I've found that young people and adults have fun learning this way.

The role-playing communication game will be the most effective if three people play.

First, one of the participants will be the presenter. The presenter must prepare a script or outline of ideas to present. Their responsibility will be to tell a story or share a thought. Mentors may provide the story or topic.

The second participant will be the listener. The listener will be responsible for demonstrating effective listening skills.

Finally, the third person is the observer. The observer will observe and document what is occurring during the conversation. They will watch the speaker and listener. Who said what? How is it said? They should have a list of the skills I have noted above as a reference. The observer's goal will be to gather as many facts (evidence) as possible to help the listener and speaker. The observer will be providing feedback to the listener and speaker.

I recommend that they provide a minimum of two positives and one recommendation. For example, the observer may share information like the feedback below.

Presenter feedback:

- Positive feedback—You presented confidently.

- Positive feedback—You had great eye contact as you spoke to the listener.

- Recommendation—I recommend that you talk a little louder.

Listener feedback:

- Positive feedback—You asked great questions to gain understanding.

- Positive feedback—You timed your responses perfectly. You never interrupted.

- Recommendation—You were leaning back in your chair. You looked a little too relaxed. I recommend that you lean slightly toward the speaker to show interest.

As mentor, you should be the facilitator and share all the responsibilities. It's important that before the game starts, everyone knows their role and is reminded about good speaking and listening fundamentals as well as the importance of remaining respectful during the game. Help participants feel comfortable and to have fun. Remind players of the game's purpose: to practice highly effective communication skills.

If you choose to have the participants write their presentations, they can start with an outline. After writing the presentation outline, give them a chance to practice it, either working with a partner or privately.

After the first round of role-playing and sharing feedback, they can change roles. Game rounds will allow each participant to be the speaker, listener, and observer.

You might find shy students not comfortable presenting. Be patient, but encourage participation. The skills they learn in the role-playing activity are life skills they will need in the future. We all need to speak, listen, and receive feedback in life. Experience can lead to communication success and continual improvement.

I have successfully used this role-playing game with groups of youth interested in learning leadership skills, and I encourage you to add this to your mentoring arsenal as well.

Chapter 11

The Self-Discipline of Endurance

E ndurance is the ability to last. People with endurance continue and remain in the fight. They don't give up. People I know who demonstrate endurance all have a can-do mindset. Most people who can endure are confident about completing what they start.

What happens if a person doesn't have the will or confidence needed for challenges? If a person thinks they can't do it, stopping is easy.

> **Learning Pursuit Pointer #11**
>
> *Endurance is the ability to last. People with endurance continue and remain in the fight. They don't give up.*

Grand Master Sung Hong Park, ninth-dan black belt in tae kwon do, was the lead instructor and owner of Park's Martial Arts in Salisbury, Maryland. He taught many different styles of martial arts, including hapkido. Hapkido is known for joint locks, pressure points, sweeps, throws, hand striking, and kicks. When a student becomes black belt in hapkido, they have self-defense skills for life. The person also had to have demonstrated endurance.

Grand Master Park shared his observation that for every Park's Martial Arts hapkido black belt, ninety-nine students enrolled in hapkido classes never attained black belt status. He didn't make this comment in boast. Grand Master Park had a business, and his business was to teach students self-defense. Instead, he was sharing a fact. In the martial art of hapkido at Park's Martial Arts, the path to a black belt skill level was like a marathon, not a sprint.

Students in hapkido class endured training that was physically and mentally challenging. Also, for martial artists to become proficient, they had to train in martial arts for years.

Grand Master Park and his instructors influenced my life and perspective on endurance. I became an assistant instructor and later an instructor at Delaware Hapkido Martial Arts Academy. I could see firsthand how challenging it was for students to commit the time, energy, and physical demands needed to learn hapkido and apply the skills proficiently. A student's confidence increases the longer they study the art.

For most students, confidence levels improve early in training, and it's rewarding to see students move from one curriculum level to the next level. Jaydon Reap, a hapkido black belt at Delaware Hapkido Martial Arts Academy, noticed and celebrated student transitions and improvement. Jaydon shared one of his first lessons while teaching and practicing martial arts: rewards in life don't come from things given to you.

New students have to test and earn their first belt, a white belt.

Just like earning martial arts belts, it takes work and endurance to achieve things of value in life. Those things you fight for will mean much more than the things given. When not earned, that same satisfaction will not be present. When we receive something with no perceived value, will we appreciate it? Does it have value?

If accomplishments in life were easy, everybody would get the same exceptional results. People who demonstrate the self-discipline of endurance understand that they will have barriers along the way. They will hit plateaus of learning where their skill level remains the same. They know that challenges will come, and pushing forward is the way to earn rewards, more skill, and success. Those who learn how to endure and overcome challenges are the black belts of life.

Reaching exceptional results and accomplishments consistently comes from the self-discipline of endurance, which is something our mentees must learn. It isn't always the most talented person who succeeds. People with a can-do attitude and the mindset that they will not stop until they reach their goal will outperform others. They will know what it feels like to earn it.

Undeserved Accolades

Undeserved accolades or accomplishments are the enemy of endurance. People who get something for nothing are missing out on the experience of enduring to reach an achievement.

Here's an example of how an unearned award can mean nothing.

A supervisor received feedback that he was not praising his team. Because of this, he decided to acknowledge the people who worked for him.

At the end of a business meeting with the team, he pulled out a box filled to the top with certificates of achievement. Before unloading the awards, he told the group about his feedback from those he supervised: "We never feel you provide us with positive feedback." He would now take action and let the team know how much he cared about them.

He acknowledged one person after another in alphabetical order and handed each team member a certificate. Each certificate had a catchy statement of praise. He was clearly trying to be sincere, but he didn't receive the response he'd hoped for. Everyone in the room felt a little awkward. They liked the supervisor, but the accolades felt underserved because everybody received a certificate.

When everybody receives an award, recognition appears forced, and everyone sees through the good-natured attempt to praise.

In this example, the team members didn't feel they received the recognition because of their endurance, perseverance, or performance. Instead, they got an award simply for showing up.

Think of your team. Not everybody on your team deserves a trophy or certificate of accomplishment. Some team members are highly effective and deserve special recognition. Others, however, coast and certainly would not be considered outstanding examples of people who endure.

I have observed teams accomplish a specific goal together and perform at a high level of excellence. You might be on that type of team. I'm not ruling out a group recognition when it's deserving. If a team of firefighters works together to save the people's lives inside a burning building, an award to each team member might be appreciated and deserving.

When you endure and achieve positive results, you know it. You don't need a trophy. Sincere praise might be enough.

Someone ineffective might get the wrong message when they get an award for performing at a low level.

We should teach our mentees the difference between receiving something for nothing and receiving accolades for actual results. Having endurance and working toward a goal is satisfying. Receiving something for nothing isn't rewarding.

Share Your Experiences

Talk to your mentee about others who have become models of success, such as athletes, musicians, actors and actresses, business leaders, and more. Most successful people didn't get to the top by gaming the system. They had to do the work. Successful people also don't usually attain success quickly. It takes time to achieve challenging goals.

Theodore Roosevelt, the twenty-sixth president of the United States, shared thoughts about endurance experiences in a speech he gave in Paris on April 23, 1910. The speech was titled "Citizenship in a Republic."

It is not the critic who counts; not the man who points out how the strong man stumbles, or where the doer of deeds could have done them better. The credit belongs to the man who is actually in the arena, whose face is marred by dust and sweat and blood; who strives valiantly; who errs, and comes short again and again, because there is no effort without error and shortcoming; but who does actually strive to do the deeds; who knows the great enthusiasms, the great devotions; who spends himself in a worthy cause; who at the best knows in the end the triumph of high achievement, and who at the worst, if he fails, at least fails while daring greatly, so that his place shall never be with those cold and timid souls who know neither victory nor defeat.

You have to be *in the arena* to get results. People who have never experienced endurance look from the outside and may never know what those who struggle have to overcome. Unfortunately, they are missing out on an opportunity.

When our mentees make mistakes, we should treat the situation as a teaching opportunity. Successful people have to overcome obstacles and learn from their mistakes. Patience and endurance are critical. The best things in life don't happen without rigorous effort in the achievement process. We need to earn it.

Endurance was a self-discipline component that Grand Master Park required. Most students didn't stick with the training long enough to achieve high success. He knew that there would be success costs for each student. The cost might be time, blood, sweat, and pain. I knew most of the black belts, and none of them ever felt that the effort and endurance needed was wasted.

You can't take your eyes off the target of your goal when things start to get tough. While taking on new challenges, we can apply the same endurance principles learned from other experiences. We can be role models for our mentees. We must consider how we overcame challenges to meet goals and share those experiences with our mentees.

Some youth may not yet have experienced endurance situations. Value systems are different for each of us. You can influence your mentee by showing them how endurance makes a difference. You can identify people practicing endurance and also identify people in history who have demonstrated endurance to achieve goals.

As we coach our mentees, we can acknowledge their efforts and recognize them as they practice the vital life skill of endurance.

Since good mentors lead by example, think of how you can demonstrate and model endurance. By modeling a skill, we go beyond storytelling and into practical application.

Build Trust

Many mentors have stories of overcoming challenges through endurance. Those stories should also be a part of the mentoring process.

Overwhelmingly, the mentors I talk to have lived through turbulent and traumatic situations, which for some is the very reason they become a mentor. Mentors could tell stories about broken homes, bad relationships, poverty, homelessness, drug and alcohol abuse, and more. These mentors have unique opportunities and can share how they overcame personal challenges and endured to succeed.

Although they may have mental scars, the mentor who understands endurance can find ways to navigate life's obstacles. Mentees may be dealing with the same types of challenging situations. Mentors need to find appropriate ways to share their experiences. This type of sharing also leads to trust.

Building a trusting relationship is another component of the mentoring process that takes time and endurance. Mentors should be patient in the trust-building process. Trust usually doesn't come quickly.

How does the self-discipline of endurance link to trust? The ability to build a trusting relationship depends on the people involved. Even if the mentoring relationship appears to be on good terms, the trust might not be there.

A sure way to build trust is to follow through on your promises. If you make a promise, keep it. If you promise to meet, be there on time. If you promise to take your mentee to an event, go to the event. Other people in their life may not follow through, but you must. Don't miss this teaching opportunity.

Your mentee may let you down at times. This doesn't mean that you break the relationship. Other people may have ended a relationship with your mentee because of disappointing situations, but I recommend mentors stick with the mentoring process. In doing this, you will demonstrate endurance while teaching through mentee mistakes.

When a mentee isn't living up to your expectations, reteach the expectations. Show them that quitting isn't an option. Be courageous and share advice.

Why am I emphasizing that you show endurance in a not-perfect relationship? So many young people have had experiences with adults who quickly gave up on them and cut off the relationship. Youth have expressed that they don't believe most adults will be around for very long, some even challenging the relationship to see if the adult is sincere. Youth don't jump into trusting relationships because many adults leave them when things get tough. Demonstrate endurance and stick around for your mentee, even in the hard times.

Reteaching Expectations

Setting expectations at the beginning of the mentoring relationship is a fundamental standard that will help make the mentorship last. All highly effective teachers know that you need to teach and reteach expectations. We can learn from this teaching strategy.

I talked to a family member who fed birds by filling a bird feeder. The bird feeder was a favorite for a variety of birds, and his yard was a favorite stop for birds for years. One day he stopped, and the birds went somewhere else.

According to expert bird watchers, birds will return to bird feeders if there is feed. What happens when birdseed is no longer available? The birds stop visiting the yard. Instead, they find other bird feeders or places where food is available.

The same thing will happen to the youth that we mentor. If we stop reteaching expectations, young people will not meet our expectations. We need to refill the bird feeder constantly with birdseed (expectations). In other words, we need to endure and reteach. Without the refilling of expectations in the minds of the young person, they start to lose focus.

What if you set an expectation of meeting on time, yet your mentee is usually late? Becoming angry and showing disappointment may not be the best way to solve the problem.

Instead of anger or, worse yet, ending the mentorship, reteach the expectation. Why is your mentee late? Help them develop routines and schedules. Keep things simple, but look for solutions. Don't give up. I've found that most of the problem with youth showing up late to events or meetings has to do with the adult, not the youth. The parent needs to get the youth to the event on time.

By not giving up and reteaching expectations, we send a message to our mentees. Not only will they know that expectations are important, but they will also learn by observing endurance in practice.

Listen for Other Endurance Activities

Always look for other experiences where trust and endurance live. You might find extracurricular opportunities to be the perfect learning experience. Our mentees can learn perseverance by participating.

As a principal, I met with parents and students regularly to discuss academic progress. During those meetings, I would ask about more than academics. Was their child involved in athletics, clubs, or other extracurricular activities? I saw how participation in different activities had positive effects on young people.

We also sponsored events to share ideas for academic success. Our school open house events were an example of a general event to share ideas. I shared my belief that young people need to be involved. Clubs, sports, and other activities are opportunities to develop self-discipline, endurance, teamwork, and much more.

My goal was for each student in the school to find some activity they could participate in and enjoy. When young people don't find activities or organizations they're passionate about, harmful activities can creep into their lives.

After open house events and assemblies with students and parents, some students came to me and offered suggestions about activities that were not available in our school. I enjoyed helping them plan and organize new clubs. If the students were passionate about a club or activity, I tried to find a sponsor and help them start the club.

At John Dickinson High School in Delaware, a few students wanted to organize a skateboard club. Other principal colleagues recommended not having this type of club on campus. They were concerned about liability but didn't see the enthusiasm from the students. I decided to approve the club because student passion for skateboarding outweighed concerns. In addition, by forming the club, the students learned how to organize and work with adults. Student leaders took the initiative. They were starting a club, and they embraced the opportunity.

The club was a success. The local newspaper even ran an article about how unique a skateboard club was in our school. The benefits to students outweighed any downsides.

While adults supported the skateboard club, students established it. As a principal, I saw youth excitement and leadership firsthand. Though we adults might be excited about certain activities, sports teams, and clubs, that doesn't mean that youth are excited about those same things. Their interests and excitement should be vital to us.

Let's remain observant and listen closely to youth, letting them choose activities that link to their interests. These are excellent opportunities to learn self-discipline principles and endurance. If they are not excited about activities, they may not invest the same energy to succeed and learn.

Set Endurance Standards

Quitting right away when things become challenging is the opposite of endurance. We must help young people set endurance standards.

Throughout my career in education, I enjoyed coaching and attending athletic events. It was an excellent way for me to get to know the students. There were always a few students who would join a club or sports team and almost immediately quit. They would stop for various reasons. Sometimes they didn't like the coach. Sometimes they didn't like the physical challenges that came with the sport. Sometimes they quit because they disliked others in the club or on the team.

We should try to avoid allowing quick quitting. I recommend that mentors and parents set a standard. Communicate clearly to the youth that immediately quitting after starting isn't an option. Set the standard of how long a youth should participate. For sports, this might be easy.

The standard for sports might be no quitting for the season. At the end of the season, if it didn't work out, that's a good time to evaluate whether or not it makes sense to try out for the next season. If they're not passionate about a sport after trying it, it may not fit their personality or abilities. However, if the standard is to complete the season, the young person will learn something about endurance.

What if they don't like the people on the team or even their coach? That's a great learning opportunity. I have yet to meet an adult who has liked everyone they've ever worked with or for. When this happens, will we quit? Probably not. We endure.

Not liking your teammates or coaches doesn't mean that you quit. This is a part of life and an opportunity to learn how to navigate dealing with people. Our mentees need this opportunity because it will not end in their youth.

By setting an endurance standard, you're teaching self-discipline. We all do things that we don't like to do. Learning to overcome challenges for personal growth can be very rewarding, and learning to experience challenges through clubs and sports is a fantastic way to experience the rewards firsthand.

Are there any exceptions to my recommendation of setting the standard of not quitting? Probably. However, look for strategies to endure the struggle.

I've met with many parents who were unhappy with their child's grades. They did the right thing and set standards for grades, including academic standards before permitting sports participation.

When things were not going well academically, some parents would become emotional and tell the student they were no longer on the team. This was the right of the parent. They were following through on the requirement of good grades. However, I always appreciated meeting with the parents early, before they removed their child from the team. Early interventions allowed us to change academic behaviors.

For example, might the student improve with extra academic time? The student could improve by receiving tutoring time. Some students improve with teacher accommodations (changing learning activities to get the same learning outcomes). Other students did much better academically when formal academic checks or contracts were in place. After providing these types of interventions, I always supported the parent. It was their decision. But I was happy to see when a student could stay in a program and experience how to overcome obstacles.

Your mentee's life may be out of balance. It may be challenging for them to engage in extracurricular activities. Extracurricular activities might not even be available. However, endurance principles are still important.

Look Out for Obstacles

Experiencing endurance and having the self-discipline to overcome obstacles is an opportunity. Think about your life accomplishments or failures. Those who have achieved superior results in their lives can almost certainly point out the road to success. Results come from the courage to push forward. It may not be easy, but you move forward.

While considering some of those wins or losses in your life, think about what might not have happened if you had not taken action. Share your experiences with your mentee. They can learn from your wins and losses.

Failing and failing again with the same mistakes doesn't improve a person's life. We all need to learn from our failures and then adjust. Endurance will not be enough without the adjustments.

Your mentee may be preparing for a transition to college or a career. In both cases, college admissions personnel or hiring personnel will be impressed by those who have demonstrated endurance. College admissions staff want to enroll people who will graduate. With no history of pushing through a challenge, they will question the person's ability to persevere.

The same is true for employers looking for employees. They want people who have demonstrated that they can get results and overcome challenges.

We should strive to teach our mentees the benefits of jumping into life situations to make them stronger. Those who don't sit on the sidelines of life have countless opportunities. The mindset of enduring and never giving up during the struggles of those opportunities will lead to even more possibilities.

Chapter 12

Determination

I have known many purpose-driven and determined people who have endured and overcome obstacles. This type of person most likely makes good decisions, focuses on outcomes from their decisions, and lets nothing get in their way.

Jesse Owens, famous American track and field athlete, exemplified extraordinary determination. Owens was a determined athlete who proved he could win. His focus was on Olympic gold during the 1936 Olympic Games, where he won four gold medals in track and field. Owens said, "We all have dreams. But in order to make dreams come into reality, it takes an awful lot of determination, dedication, self-discipline, and effort" (Jesse Owens Memorial Park Links and Facts, accessed June 15, 2023).

Jesse Owens was a gifted athlete, but thousands of talented athletes in the world wanted to compete and win in the 1936 Olympic Games. Owens had a dream of winning in the Olympics, but he knew he could not just rely on his athletic talent. He had the self-discipline to prepare in advance. He made decisions and demonstrated endurance.

As an African American in 1936, Jesse Owens endured racism before, during, and after the Olympic Games. Even with those added pressures, there was no stopping his dreams and drive. No social barriers were going to stop him. He decided to do whatever it took to represent the United States of America in the Olympics.

People with determination anticipate enduring hardships and challenges. They maintain their focus when the challenges come.

Learning Pursuit Pointer #12

People with determination anticipate enduring hardships and challenges. They maintain their focus when the challenges come.

As we work with mentees, it's important to share how determination closely links to endurance. When observed in action, the self-discipline of determination can lead to exceptional results.

Determination requires a purpose. For Jesse Owens, the purpose was to win in the Olympics. Without a purpose and focus, actions linking to the determination mindset may not get the person to where they want to go.

Determined people can appear passionate about achieving goals or may not appear emotional but still steadfast. The personality of the determined person can vary.

People with determination are not always successful, but they make decisions and stick with them. They are not distracted by the next shiny object. By understanding and living determination principles, outcomes improve. A person who makes good decisions and then follows through on those decisions demonstrates courage and determination.

Different Value Systems

For some mentees, their value system might not include a practical perspective about determination. Their experiences in society and family may not include observation of determination.

Your mentee may have only observed family members who made decisions and then changed course. They may only be familiar with people who are not consistent. When your role models are constantly changing decisions, you might become the same type of decision-maker.

Can we make our mentees courageous decision-makers who demonstrate determination? Determination will affect their future.

Employers look for people who demonstrate determination. College admissions staff want to enroll people who have decision-making and determination skills. They want to find people who finish what they start.

Within families, determination could be an honored family tradition. Some families teach that determination leads to success. However, other young people may not have role models who demonstrate determination. Value systems will vary, which may require you to adjust how you teach determination.

In the following scenarios, look for the differences in value systems.

Anthony

You mentor sixteen-year-old Anthony. He and his younger brother live with their mother, but they live close to many other family members in the community. His father isn't actively involved in his life.

As far as Anthony knows, no one in his family has ever graduated from high school. Several family members are unemployed, and those who are employed work in low-paying jobs. From his perspective, employment opportunities provide an opportunity to survive.

While discussing his family, he shares that most of his family members are not excited about working. They have an attitude that says their goal is to make it through the day. Anthony has observed family members leaving their jobs only to move on to other low-paying jobs. Overall, he sees behaviors signaling little drive or pride in work.

His mother is the exception. When he talks about his mother, it's clear that she is his role model. She has a different perspective. Although survival is essential, she constantly talks to Anthony about the importance of doing the job well. The same employer has employed her for ten years. She is a mentor to new staff and is determined to ensure they are gaining skills and growing on the job.

Anthony sees her determination, responsible decision-making, and drive to help others. Anthony and his mother talk about those characteristics of highly effective employees.

Anthony's mother and other family members talk about the benefits of education, but no one in his family has followed through and benefited from the educational system. They would like to see Anthony graduate from high school and go to college. His mom constantly talks about his potential. Although she doesn't attend school events, she demonstrates the importance of education by checking his academic progress. She is an engaged parent.

Anthony's mom is the leader of the family. She is determined to help her family survive. She loves her family members and will do whatever it takes to get them through any challenges. In addition, Anthony's mother supports his dream of going to college for engineering.

Cynthia

Cynthia is also a sixteen-year-old high school student and has two younger siblings. She has a mother and father, but in her words, "they don't get along." Both have college degrees. Cynthia doesn't have any other relatives who live close to her.

Her mother works as a retail manager. She has worked her way into management by getting results in her profession. Even though she has a college degree, she continues taking classes to prepare for future opportunities.

Her father also is in a leadership position. He works in a transportation company. At his job, he supervises a team responsible for distributing products throughout the United States. He also learns skills that might lead to promotions or a change to a higher-paying job.

Cynthia's parents believe that education will provide opportunities for their children. They participate fully in the school's parent organization. Staff at the school know Cynthia's parents by name.

Her parents are extremely busy. There are sometimes brief family discussions during transitions from one activity to the next. The family is always on the go. Cynthia has learned the importance of determination by watching her parents, but the family spends little time together.

Cynthia's parents love their children just like Anthony's mom loves him, but Cynthia's parents don't spend much time with them. They are determined to prepare their children for college opportunities and skills needed for future success. Her parents are unaware that Cynthia doesn't want to go to college. She wants to find a career opportunity in online technology, an entry-level position where she can learn technology skills.

Big Dreams

Through family members, Anthony and Cynthia have witnessed determination in practice. However, the value systems are different. One family focuses on survival at all costs. The other family does things to survive but focuses on activities that will lead to promotion.

Anthony and Cynthia have parents who care for them, but a mentor might need to fine-tune learning opportunities about determination for each youth. What can they take from their family experiences to fine-tune their determination skills? The learning will need to include a perspective on how they plan to achieve their goals and their dreams.

While working with early adolescent student athletes, I often would ask what they wanted to do after high school. What were their dreams? Not surprisingly, many athletes would tell me they wanted to play professional sports. I didn't discourage their dreams, but I would have a deeper conversation with them.

Professional and Olympic athletes usually participate in college-level sports before becoming professional athletes. The young athletes would agree that this was a logical next step that they would have to take to achieve their goals. What is the path to college enrollment and participation in sports at the college level? Many of the young people didn't know the answer.

If your mentee has a dream that will be extremely hard to achieve, what should you do? Provide facts.

The math doesn't look good for people who want to play professional sports. However, criticizing a young person's dream will not help the mentor-and-mentee relationship. With that said, it's still important to be realistic about the situation.

The National Collegiate Athletic Association (NCAA) is a member-led organization that communicates a vision of dedication to college athletes' well-being and lifelong success. According to the NCAA, the probability of top college-level athletes moving on to professional sports is very low. They back up their low transition to professional sports with data.

For 2020, the NCAA calculated probability statistics for football, baseball, basketball, and ice hockey. In those sports, very few participants were drafted into professional teams. For example, of the 73,212 athletes who participated in NCAA football, only 254 were drafted into the professional league. Basketball was similar. Of the 16,509 basketball players, the professional basketball league drafted only thirty-one players.

When mentoring a youth who wants to play professional basketball, don't hide those statistics. Those types of statistics provide an opportunity for research and discussion about the future. I recommend that mentors share with mentees that even the most determined super athlete may not hit the target of professional sports or the Olympics. That doesn't mean that they shouldn't try.

It would be surprising to find professional athletes or Olympians who didn't demonstrate endurance and determination. We want our mentees to learn those self-discipline principles.

How do top athletes reach their goals? Challenge the mentee to research this question by looking at individual athletes. What have others done to accomplish the level of success desired? Are there similar attributes? For example, physical attributes are important in athletics. However, there must be much more. Most elite college athletes are gifted physically. There are other differences between professional-level athletes and others who are just as strong, agile, and fast.

Diversification

Squirrels are determined, but squirrels have limitations. When plan A doesn't work, they go to plan B.

I enjoy nature and learn all I can from going outside and observing nature in action. I live close to forest areas, where raccoons, deer, birds, and a community of Eastern gray squirrels visit my backyard. The squirrels and birds are my most visible neighbors.

For fun, I feed squirrels and birds. Squirrels love the peanuts that I share with them in the mornings. The birds enjoy the bird feeder. Squirrels are not satisfied with peanuts. They want the bird feed.

When I started feeding birds, I used a flatbed feeder. A shepherd's hook pole suspended the feeder. The feeder was open to any critter that could get to the platform holding the feed. I placed the bird feeder in an open space in my yard.

Squirrels are extreme superhero athletic creatures, especially the Eastern gray squirrels in my backyard. Although small, they can leap approximately nine feet horizontally and four feet vertically. Because of their athletic ability and natural determination, my bird feeder was no match for their focus on food.

I watched the squirrels climb the pole quickly to access the birdseed. They didn't even need to use their leaping ability. They just climbed up the pole.

I was determined to stop this attack on the bird feeder, so I decided to try one strategy after another. Each strategy failed as the squirrels were able to overcome my obstacles. I built mechanical slides around the pole with bungee cords and springs. If squirrels could laugh, they would have laughed at me. My mechanical effort didn't work. Squirrels have precise body control and could always outmaneuver my efforts. The squirrels were more determined than my plan to stop them. Each time I tried a new strategy, it failed.

Most squirrels figured out ways around all the mechanisms I put on the pole. However, I saw squirrels bypassing the pole and leaping from trees to access the birdseed. It was as if they were showing me more than one way to get around my thinking. They were successful.

I was amazed at how determined the squirrels were to get to the food. Finally, I found that others had identified a squirrel's weaknesses to keep them from bird feeders: size and weight.

I purchased a bird feeder that closes an opening to the birdseed when squirrels put weight on the platform. Their size prevented them from defying gravity, but I was amazed at the determination of the squirrels to get around that problem. They were problem-solving after each failure.

They climbed the pole to strategically try to decrease the amount of weight they put on the platform. I watched them leap extraordinary distances to the platform. They thought coming in from a high vantage point might help them solve the problem. I watched squirrels sitting on the fence, studying the bird feeder. The same squirrel would move to a different location and study again. The squirrels were determined to figure out how to solve the weight problem that cut off their birdseed supply. This went on for days. They were determined to win the challenge.

After approximately one week, the squirrels no longer tried to get to the seed. All their determination and strategies seemed to come to an end. Although highly determined, the reality of the problem took over.

Now the squirrels scurry underneath the bird feeder and eat the small amounts of birdseed that drop to the ground from the birds.

We can all learn from the Eastern gray squirrel. Their determination is impressive. However, even the athletic and highly gifted problem-solving squirrel will understand there is a time to change direction. Climbing, contorting, and diving at a bird feeder didn't work, so they chose a different path and found food elsewhere.

Many great athletes navigate their way to the top in college-level sports, where they're just about to break through to become a professional athlete or Olympian, and then it happens—a career-ending injury destroys their athletic goals. It can happen to any athlete. If the total investment were in becoming a professional athlete, the future would be unclear after a career-ending injury. Many have asked, "What am I going to do now?"

Mentors should provide a path to actions that will take the mentee to more than one outcome. The mentee needs to be able to see how a career plan can identify the following:

- Primary goal (first career choice)

- Secondary goal (second career choice)

- Attributes needed to accomplish both goals (diversification)

- Actions required now to achieve both goals

- Completion date (short-term)

These variables can be written for the mentee in a plan and discussed. This is a great way to teach the art of diversification as we reach for our dreams.

Chapter 13

Willpower

Could you survive a stampede? If so, could you survive a wave of stampedes? One after another, here they come. Do you have the willpower to survive?

Imagine the African grasslands. A great herd of wildebeests and zebras spread out in a picturesque scene. The landscape looks like paradise. There are thousands of animals in the herd, and they graze quietly in the grasslands. The backdrop is a sky filled with white, puffy cumulus clouds and a far-off mountain. The sun is just starting to drop closer to the horizon, which brings a pinkish-red color to the sky. What a beautiful view!

Suddenly, everything changes. You hear stress-filled cries coming from animals as they alert each other that a predator is nearby. Unrest spreads like an out-of-control fire through the herd. The eyes of the animals become alert and search for threats. Heads are held high, and nostrils breathe in and out at a quicker rate. The noise is frightening because of the size of the herd. The animals seem to be looking in your direction as a path away from danger. Since you're standing in open grassland, the herds gallop and then sprint toward you and away from what they perceive as danger. You now have an immediate problem: stampede!

Do you have the willpower to survive? Willpower is the strength of the mind. Has your mind been conditioned for strength or challenging situations like a stampede? Has your mentee had experiences of success due to willpower? Would you instinctively have the strength of mind to evaluate your situation (problem-solve), or would only responses such as fight-or-flight manifest?

Hopefully, you will never encounter a stampede, but I'm positive that you have faced many challenges. We can enhance our willpower by experiencing, preparing for, and overcoming challenges. Just like there are options in surviving a stampede, we have options available to overcome day-to-day challenges in life. Having the willpower—the strength of mind—will influence outcomes.

The Human Brain

In *The Owner's Manual for the Brain: The Ultimate Guide to Peak Mental Performance at All Ages*, author Pierce J. Howard, PhD, (2014) describes a fantastic characteristic of the human brain. More than half of the human brain is uncommitted to synapses and networks, so half of our brain is available for forming new synapses and networks. We have enormous opportunities to be creative, problem-solve, analyze, and improve memory.

Upon examining the human brain, the cerebral cortex is the outermost layer. Gray matter makes up the cerebral cortex. The cerebral cortex allows humans to think critically. For the purpose of this illustration, understand that the cerebral cortex is a brain part that separates humans from animals. Our brains are unique.

Since we have a moment before the stampede of animals arrives, I will describe a special system in the brain and a part of the brain that might help save us from the crushing effects of a stampede.

There are two amygdala in the human limbic system, which controls several cognitive and emotional functions. The amygdala is an almond-shaped cell cluster at the base of the brain that primarily controls emotions, memory, and fight-or-flight response. It is a complex part of the brain with many more functions, but as we deal with a stampede, we need a well-functioning amygdala.

As we observe the stampede, our amygdala communicates with the hypothalamus, also in the limbic system. The hypothalamus communicates with the autonomic nervous system. Without us controlling the brain communication system, the stampede will automatically elevate emotions.

In his book *Brain-based Learning: The New Paradigm of Teaching*, author Eric P. Jensen (2008, 48) shares, "Under threat, the brain uses less of the reflective higher-order thinking skills of the frontal lobe and resorts to using more of the reflexive nature of the amygdala."

The brain is a part of the central nervous system. The central nervous system also includes the spinal cord. In addition to the central nervous system, we have a peripheral nervous system. The peripheral nervous system includes nerves that branch out from the brain and spinal cord and extend to other parts of the body, like muscles and organs. Both systems are vital in body communication.

As we consider our response to a stampede, we must look closer at the peripheral nervous system. Within the peripheral nervous system, there is the autonomic nervous system. This part of the nervous system regulates involuntary body functions such as blood flow, heartbeat, digestion, and breathing. These bodily functions are not under your control. Instead, they are automatic.

There are two nervous systems within the autonomic system: parasympathetic and sympathetic.

The parasympathetic systems allow us to operate in a normal state without thinking or controlling our body functions. In this state, we conserve physical energy without thinking. For example, we don't have to think about our blood flow. The parasympathetic system takes care of this bodily function. Before the stampede, your parasympathetic system was in a normal state of operation.

Our sympathetic systems regulate our bodies during environmental stress. Environmental stress might be a stampede coming in your direction. This state is the fight-or-flight response.

When you see the stampede charging your way, your heart rate will accelerate, your breathing rate will increase, more blood will flow to your muscles, your pupils will dilate, and sweat secretion will activate. When your sympathetic system engages, the cerebral cortex, the problem-solving part of your brain, stops working. According to Dr. Howard, instinct and training take over (2014).

These human systems are amazing. Unlike the wildebeest and zebra charging in a stampede, our human brains can think critically. We can learn the benefits of having willpower. Even in emergencies, our human brain can function beyond an animal instinct reaction. However, in a stampede, you will be reacting to a threat, and your brain will work differently. If you have the training to escape charging animals, that information will help you survive.

Having willpower in a survival situation will be advantageous with an oncoming wildebeest-and-zebra stampede. Strength of mind means that you will find whatever way possible to survive. A person with willpower will utilize the fight-or-flight response and experiences learned in the past.

I've not gone through extensive training on outrunning wildebeest and zebra. I have watched television shows where I can see the extreme athleticism of those beasts, and I'm certain that in a race, I would lose 100 percent of the time. I can rule out outrunning the herd. They will catch me if I use that strategy. With that said, I know that I may need to go from point A to point B quickly, so I would have to run if I wanted to survive.

If you're physically strong, do you have options for using your strength against the herd? I'm speaking to all the weightlifters reading this book. Will powerlifters have an advantage against the herd? No human has the strength to meet a herd of zebra and wildebeest head-on. The momentum of the herd will overpower a strong person in seconds, but having strength, just like the ability to run, might help in an escape.

In addition to being fast and strong, we might be able to identify several other attributes that will help us survive a stampede.

When faced with a stampede, I would confidently say I am missing an attribute to stay alive. I have never received training on how to survive a stampede. Imagine how much more confident I would be if an expert had trained me to survive this significant challenge.

Three Options

Richard Johnson (2012, 045) identifies outdoor survival actions in *The Ultimate Survival Manual: 333 Skills That Will Get You Out Alive*. Surviving a stampede is a topic in the book in which he recommends three strategies that may help you survive: look around for a barrier, dive in the water, or act as an obstacle.

First, we should look for barriers where we can conceal our bodies away from the herd. A tree or rock barrier might be close enough for us to reach before the thunderous hooves reach our location. Being physically fit and able to run or climb might provide an advantage. If we have trained our bodies to be physically fit before the stampede, we might have a better chance of survival.

Diving into water is another strategy to avoid a stampede. Most stampeding animals don't venture into the water. However, Johnson also points out that water could have other dangers. Remember, we are in Africa in this scenario. The water might be the home of hungry crocodiles. Our training before the stampede hopefully provided additional information about how to survive a crocodile attack. I don't have crocodile attack training, but I feel confident that one of the survival strategies would be not to jump into a body of water where they live.

Finally, the third option is to act as an obstacle. A trained survivalist understands the nature of stampeding animals. Most stampeding animals instinctively don't want to break or injure their legs by stepping on rocks or logs. In most cases, they will jump over obstacles to avoid injuries that could turn them into easy prey. If you make yourself look like a log or rock, an obvious obstacle to the animal, they will hopefully jump over you.

Although a stampede is a unique example of survival and overcoming a challenge, we can identify other challenges in life where willpower is needed to succeed. We have the unique ability to use our brains. We are problem solvers, yet we still have a physical switch that will help us survive by the fight-or-flight response. With willpower, survival and success are much more likely.

As we mentor, we need to make our mentees aware of the powers of willpower. We must provide them with training that will strengthen their minds—this will show them how to prepare for the unexpected. Experiences where they overcome obstacles will provide a template for future challenges.

As I described willpower in this section, I went into detail about how the mind works, though I tried to keep it simple. The science of the brain is extremely complex, and experts still argue over precisely what is happening in our brains at any given time. I know that our mind is much more than simple systems that work. We can problem-solve and plan for the future. People with superior willpower are much more successful in the success process, even if they don't understand the brain's complexity and how it works.

The opposite is true if a person doesn't have willpower. Someone without willpower may just immediately give up. They may take the consequences of being trampled by the herd. Can you think of people in your life who gave up just before the possibility of success? The person might not understand the principle of willpower. They go along without making choices, no matter the perceived outcome. If the result is negative, so be it. They don't understand the innate power of their mind.

We should look for principles of willpower. As mentors, we are responsible for providing examples and opportunities for mentees to practice and observe willpower in action. By doing this, they will know that they can accomplish much with the proper mindset.

In the stampede scenario, survival seems possible with the will to survive and knowledge of how to survive a stampede. The survival rate will expand if you have trained for a stampede situation. All wild beasts are effortlessly jumping over our bodies; I can see it now. Sharp hooves are inches away from our covered heads. Although stressful, we survive but don't relax too soon. Something was chasing the herd. Do you have the willpower to meet the next challenge? We can do this!

Language

Choice of language affects willpower. I believe that language can affect a person's strength of mind or willpower. Think of the people in your life who have a can-do attitude. How do they compare to the people who constantly communicate that they can't do it? Language is important. I believe it even affects how you think. Through my military experience, I learned a technique to get rid of unwanted language.

We were several days into basic training, all still trying to get used to the changes in our lives as United States Air Force recruits. The military training instructors (drill sergeants) were using various teaching methods, one of which was to come very close to you, face-to-face, and scream directions. For some, this teaching method was effective in changing our habits. Others took a little longer, and they were subject to a different teaching strategy.

As soon as we arrived at Lackland Air Force Base, we received an order to respond to all instructors with a respectful acknowledging statement. If one asked me a question, I would respond by coming to attention and stating, "Sir (or ma'am), Airman Carmack reports as ordered." After this statement, I could follow with an answer or comment.

The required response might seem simple and easy to accomplish, but many eighteen-year-old recruits quickly responded inappropriately. They used civilian responses used throughout their lives. Many forgot our ordered response and responded quickly, "Yeah." The training instructors didn't like the word "yeah," and when they didn't like something, everyone could tell. They weren't putting on a show, either; they were genuinely upset. We observed them turn red and begin to sweat. They always moved closer to you while transitioning from neutral (they never appeared happy) to angry.

One of the recruits in our dorm continually made the mistake of saying "yeah" when responding to the lead training instructor. After several days of errors, it continued. I thought I would see the teaching strategy of moving close and yelling. However, that clearly wasn't working, so the instructor used a different teaching method.

With over three decades as an educator, I never utilized his teaching method, but it seemed to work in the military barracks.

Before I go any further, unless you're training military recruits, never use this unusual teaching strategy. Most people will intuitively know this, but this is a warning just in case.

We were all in the dormitory area when the training instructor could take no more. After the eighteen-year-old recruit responded with a "yeah" once more, a screaming training instructor ordered the recruit to go directly into the latrine area.

While yelling in the recruit's face, they ran to the latrine, where the instructor scolded the recruit over and over again about his improper response. The rest of us had no idea what might be coming next. And though we couldn't see inside the latrine area, we were listening closely.

While banging on the toilet stall barriers, the instructor ordered the recruit to open a toilet lid and scream "yeah" repeatedly into the toilet. The recruit obeyed but wasn't yelling loudly enough to satisfy the instructor; so the instructor ordered him to yell "yeah" louder into the toilet. The recruit screamed "yeah" repeatedly while the instructor screamed at him and banged on the stall wall.

It occurred to the rest of us during the situation that this was rather funny. I am sure the recruit, under the watchful eye of the training instructor at the time, was not amused. After screaming "yeah" into a toilet for what seemed an eternity, the instructor screamed out, "Now flush them!" The recruit flushed the toilet, and I visualized the "yeahs" going down the toilet.

This intense discarding of the word "yeah" continued for a few flushes. Finally, it all ended abruptly. The training instructor briskly left the latrine and recruit area. The unfortunate recruit followed with a new mindset and a smile, and we all began to laugh at the situation.

I don't recall him ever making the mistake of responding with a "yeah" again. We all learned from the experience, and very few "yeahs" came out of our mouths from that point on.

I found a letter from our commander at Lackland Air Force Base, a letter I was given on the first day of basic training. In the letter, the commander pointed out that "we would be tested physically, emotionally, mentally, and spiritually in order to bring out the best." The commander also said we should "keep things in perspective and don't lose your sense of humor" (M. G. Armstrong).

The latrine situation was humorous. Even the recruit who experienced personal time with the training instructor laughed after the training instructors left the area.

I don't recommend that we treat our mentees the way the military training instructors treat recruits. Basic military training is unique. However, I recommend that we teach our mentees the importance of language and how our minds work.

Learning Pursuit Pointer #13

People with positive thoughts and language set themselves up for success. It isn't a guarantee, but optimistic language makes a difference.

Change the word "yeah" to two words I often hear, "I can't." We should flush those two words down the toilet. People with positive thoughts and language set themselves up for success. It isn't a guarantee, but optimistic language makes a difference.

People who push thoughts of "I can't" out of their minds (mentally flushing them down the toilet) and instead have thoughts of "I can" still experience challenges. However, they choose not to engage in negative thoughts. If negative thoughts manifest, positive thinkers understand the benefit of looking for the positive path.

I have enjoyed working with people who believe they can get things done. For example, when working with children from poverty, some educators thought optimistically about the teaching process. They were confident they could change the lives of children. They constantly communicated that we could get the job done—student academic achievement. They backed optimism up with actions and teaching skills. Those children under the care of optimistic and highly effective teachers had the best chance of learning.

As mentors, we need to constantly help our mentees with their mindset. When they say they can't do something, we must ensure they understand that language will undoubtedly assist them in an unsatisfactory outcome. We need to model for them an optimistic perspective. This mentoring helps a mentee see how willpower flourishes with a can-do attitude.

Flush "I can't" thoughts and language down the toilet. "I can" is the language used by people with extraordinary willpower.

Chapter 14

The Power of Hope

I hope I've made a good case on why you need to share the importance of endurance, determination, and willpower as a mentor. Most of us can identify people in our lives who have demonstrated how these self-discipline components help overcome obstacles. With them, our mentees will be on the path to success.

In the best-selling book *Man's Search for Meaning*, written by psychiatrist Dr. Viktor E. Frankl (1946), the subject of hope was an unavoidable topic. Dr. Frankl was a prisoner in Nazi death camps where he experienced unimaginable horrors. In concentration camps, superior physical attributes didn't guarantee survival. However, Dr. Frankl discovered that hope and survival were linked.

Dr. Frankl noticed that when people lost hope for the future, they lost the will to live. He wrote, "The prisoner who had lost faith in the future—his future—was doomed. With his loss of belief in the future, he also lost his spiritual hold; he let himself decline and became subject to mental and physical decay" (Frankl 1946, 95).

Even though we all have or will experience some darkness in our lives, most of us can't even imagine the overwhelming stress of being a prisoner in a concentration camp. However, we can still apply some of the fundamental concepts learned and taught by Dr. Frankl.

When we or our mentees encounter a dark time in life—addiction, homelessness, abuse, medical challenges, loss, etc.—we need to reach deep into our minds and remember that we still have some power of choice.

Dr. Frankl chose to study the people around him to share his experience with others. Maybe that's what kept him alive as he encountered horror after horror. When we understand that we still have power and control in the worst circumstances, even if the control is minimal, hope will remain alive.

A Choice

Like Dr. Frankl, my mother observed the power of hope. She struggled with several medical problems toward the end of her life, requiring medical assistance in nursing homes. Although she had physical challenges, she was mentally sharp and interacted well with other patients and caregivers. Even though she was dealing with her challenges, she would find people within the facilities who needed friends. She tried to get to know and support the other patients through kind discussions about the future.

She was able to share with me the hopes and dreams of the people she met. Like her, they wanted improved health, which was the path to home and back to their families. Their families and friends were a priority. With good health, they dreamed of becoming more self-sufficient. They didn't have a dream of becoming a burden to their families.

I visited her one day, and she had a different perspective on one of the patients, a gentleman she had tried to get to know. She told me that he had been diagnosed with terminal cancer. Although the cancer was taking over his body, he still was strong of mind. She described him and his lack of hope for the future. Like the prisoners observed by Dr. Frankl, the cancer patient no longer had hope. He no longer spoke to people, nor did he want to eat. The nurses tried to change his mindset and get him to do the things necessary to go home to be with his family at the end of his life. No one could change his actions. He no longer had hope for the future. Because there was no hope, he made a choice about his life. I don't criticize his actions. It was his choice.

For the people we mentor, we must remind them how hope fuels endurance, determination, and willpower. Without that glimmer of hope, all else will seem unimportant. Life will seem unimportant.

For some, this can be a huge challenge.

Fix the Canteen

Imagine a youth that is dealing with chronic trauma in life. The physical and mental abuse never seems to end, and hope seems to be nowhere in sight. For this youth, a mentor should consider asking for help. Mental health experts have skills that mentors may not have.

Learning Pursuit Pointer #14

Hope brings clarity when challenges come in from all angles.

None of us can survive without water. Imagine how important water would be to you as you walked through a desert. If you suddenly noticed your canteen had a slow leak, would you take action? It would be time to problem-solve, time to figure out how to stop the water from leaving the canteen.

Like the water leaving the canteen, we need to take action when our mentee loses hope. We must have hope to prosper in life. When we see a mentee who seems to be losing hope, it's our responsibility to try to find a way to assist. People without hope are more challenging to fix than a hole in a canteen.

Find ways to discuss how your mentee feels about the future. What excites them? If you find no hope, fixing your mentee's "canteen" should be a priority. Help them understand how important it will be for them to keep hope alive.

Hope is an essential part of endurance, willpower, and determination. In fact, it's a driving force. Without hope, we will struggle from moment to moment. Hope brings clarity when challenges come in from all angles.

Chapter 15

Self-Control

I have had hundreds of discussions with youth about self-control. As a principal, I was responsible for the learning in my school. The only way to make sure that learning occurred was to have control of the approximately one thousand students put in my charge. Self-control was a problem for some youth, and I had to help them learn good self-control behaviors.

Chronic stress has a strong negative impact on a young person's life. Excessive stress at home affects the child at school mainly through poor attendance and declining academic performance. Chronic stress can also wreak havoc on a child's health.

I will never forget one particular student struggling with attendance, academics, and behavior. We initiated an intervention team to identify the problem with him, yet our interventions didn't affect any of these areas.

One intervention team member was responsible for visiting homes. By visiting the home, she began to learn why he always seemed to be in a state of stress: the student was highly fearful of an uncle who had threatened to kill him with a hatchet. The uncle had a history of assault, and he was well known in the community as dangerous and that he would probably use a weapon in an altercation. For this reason, our student wouldn't go home. Instead, he would go to an abandoned house and sleep in an attic crawl space.

We became aware of the situation in the middle of winter. There was no heat in his hiding spot, and he was under tremendous stress. The pressure was influencing his behavior and academics. Based on brain research, his stress could easily have affected his physical development.

Our perspective about his behavior changed. Initially, the team of teachers could not understand why he refused to do homework. After discovering the problem with his uncle, we realized that he was in a state of survival. For him, the school was not a priority.

Build Relationships

Every student sent to me with self-control problems has been different, and I saw various problems in those who lacked self-control. To identify and categorize the problem, I first had to ask questions. I knew these students would be more successful if I could change their behavior.

Even though mentors may have busy schedules, they need to take the time to build a relationship with youth.

With an established good relationship, youth might be open to feedback. With no positive relationship, change is less likely. We must find a way to make young people understand our desire to help.

Emotions varied when a student came to my office. Some of the students were angry. Other students were stressed and worried about the consequences, like a call home to mom or dad. I encountered students who didn't seem to care about their actions. Mentors may find similar emotional behaviors when working with mentees who struggle with self-control.

I always set the tone of the meetings with students, making it clear that I had high expectations for them. At the same time, I ensured that they understood that I wanted to hear their side of the problem. Why did they lack self-control? How did the situation start that sent them to the principal's office? Were there other people involved? Did they realize that they had a self-control problem?

I was interested in facts and their perspective, but if the behaviors disrupted others, I expected they would learn from the experience and make changes for the future. Lack of self-control was not setting them up for success in school or beyond.

Let your mentee know that self-control is a valued skill. As a mentor who has a great relationship with your mentee, you have an opportunity to influence their value system. Without you, the value system of a young person may not clearly show the benefits of self-control.

Mentors are not the primary influencers for young people. Parents have a responsibility to teach. Some students come from situations where they don't see role models at home. If no one at home has self-control, the youth in that home will usually not value self-control. On the other hand, some students have role models at home, yet they still lack self-control.

Build a relationship with the youth, and that will allow you to help them with self-control.

Consider Nutrition and Sleep

Adolescence (ages ten to twenty-four years) is a time of change. The body and brain change during adolescence. What happens in the brain during adolescence is amazing. Adolescence is a time when youth are transitioning to being adults. This transition time means youth change intellectually, physically, hormonally, and socially. Nutrition and sleep influence youth self-control.

Most public schools now have programs to feed students identified as living in low economic situations. It's also well accepted that nutrition could be a factor in youth development, including their brains. Students with good nutritional situations will have a better chance of learning.

Also, schools continue to focus on adolescence and sleep. Sleep is vital for everyone, but a developing adolescent brain seems to work more effectively with sleep, and according to research, sleep duration is essential for healthy children (Tarokh 2016, 182).

I have personally witnessed the negative effects of sleep deprivation on youth. Many of them arrive late to school, which is how I came to meet them. Some students spend time on the streets with their friends late at night, while others have parents who allow them to play video games all night. When parents don't exercise control over their children's sleep habits, it can lead to poor academic performance or behavioral issues.

Acknowledge the Messy Ball of Clay

Brain research supports what I saw in schools. Neurological studies have found that brain maturation during adolescence can be influenced by the environment and heredity. Mariam Arain (2013), author of a scientific journal article called "Maturation of the Adolescent Brain," explained.

> Brain maturation during adolescence (ages 10–24 years) could be governed by several factors. It may be influenced by heredity and environment, prenatal and postnatal insult, nutritional status, sleep patterns, pharmacotherapy, and surgical interventions during early childhood. Furthermore, physical, mental, economical, and psychological stress; drug abuse (caffeine, nicotine, and alcohol); and sex hormones including estrogen, progesterone, and testosterone can influence the development and maturation of the adolescent brain. (450)

When I examined academic performance, many students who didn't perform well academically grew up in low social-economic situations. Children living in poverty have more significant environmental challenges to overcome than those who do not. This isn't absolute, but it does play a role in academic success.

In the publication *Brain Facts: A Primer on the Brain and Nervous System*, the teen brain is referred to as "a big ball of clay, ready to change and be molded by new experiences—but it is also very messy" (The Society for Neuroscience 2002, 51). Why is it messy?

The prefrontal cortex is the part of the brain responsible for decision-making, critical thinking, creativity, planning, and problem-solving. The prefrontal cortex is a part of the cerebrum and is in the forehead area. We can sort through information and make good choices with our prefrontal cortex.

By the age of fifteen or sixteen, an adolescent brain will function similarly to an adult brain. According to Thomas Armstrong (2016), author of *Power of the Adolescent Brain*, there is an exception to the function similarities. Armstrong says, "The adolescent can think as maturely as an adult under laboratory conditions, or in what has been termed as cold cognitive setting—that is, in circumstances where there are no emotions or social interactions or pressures involved" (40).

The emotional part of the brain is referred to as the limbic system. The limbic system includes the following brain structures: hippocampus, amygdala, cingulate gyrus, thalamus, and hypothalamus. Around puberty the limbic system finishes developing. The limbic finishes developing before the prefrontal cortex. Armstrong (2016) points out that the prefrontal cortex, though mostly developed by midadolescence, may not function smoothly with the limbic system and other brain parts until a person's early twenties.

This information means that youth are trying to figure out the world while their brains are still developing. It's more difficult for youth to make complex decisions when they become emotional. In addition, adolescent behaviors such as risk-taking and sensation-seeking increase during the teenage year (The Society for Neuroscience 2002, 51).

Learning Pursuit Pointer #15

It's more difficult for youth to make complex decisions when they become emotional.

As mentors, we have an excellent opportunity to share brain research with others, especially our mentees. We want our mentees to learn self-control, and helping them understand brain development might significantly influence their ability to do so.

I've experienced youth in a school setting who appeared to be problem solvers, critical thinkers, and exceptional academic students when in calm situations but later witnessed something change when they became emotional. Their emotions seemed to control their behavior, taking them from a state of self-control to almost instantly in tears or excessively angry.

During my discussions with one youth who had lost self-control, I would ask them to explain what happened. After listening, sometimes I would have them write the sequence of events that led to the problem, helping us identify at what point they lost control and were no longer able to problem-solve or make good decisions.

Writing about what happened helped the youth understand and recall event sequences. Some of them were surprised at their behavior and offered suggestions for the future. A person aware of emotional triggers might be able to avoid the problem in the future. This process was better than me pointing out the problem as I saw it.

Any time we take the time to self-analyze our actions, we learn much more than someone telling us what they believe occurred. In most cases, I was not with the youth when the problem happened, so their analysis was essential.

The identification of strategies followed this process of self-analysis. I wanted them to identify strategies they could use to avoid the same problem in the future. Many of the suggestions were on target with what I would have offered. Students would often say, "I should have walked away." Others shared that they should have found a friend or come to my office to discuss the problem and find a reasonable solution.

A good strategy is to have your mentees look for solutions, which will help them in the future when similar situations occur.

I also found it beneficial to describe self-control issues when more than one person is involved. When a young person reacts to another, who is in control? Is it the person who loses control? Most of the people I was counseling pondered this question. The other person was controlling the youth who had lost self-control. After finding out they had been manipulated and controlled, they didn't want to find themselves in that situation again. They wanted to control their behaviors and not be manipulated by others.

Facilitate the Calming Process

In those office meetings, youth challenged with self-control problems could only learn self-control strategies after calming down. If they were still emotional, they might have looked like they were listening, but their minds were not processing the information effectively. Remember, we learned how adolescents will be less effective with logical thinking when emotions are high.

For some students, I set an environment in my office to allow them to calm their minds. This calming process might include allowing the students to write what occurred. Some of the students did drawings of physical locations rather than writing a description of the event. In addition, I would sometimes provide them with flowcharts to help them organize their thoughts. Some of the students needed to move physically. I would sometimes accompany a student on a walk around the building as we solved the problem.

Celebrate Victories

When youth make corrections and change behavior, it's a time for celebration. For students who changed their self-control behavior, simple words of congratulation made a difference. I would sometimes even celebrate by contacting the parents of those students who had improved.

Some of the best celebrations occurred when I observed a student controlling their behavior during a stressful situation. I followed up with praise and acknowledged success. When you see those little changes, it's time to praise.

Students who had severe self-control problems changed their behavior in small ways. These small changes began to become more significant victories. I acknowledged the small changes first. For example, if I was working with a student with self-control issues and observed that student actively engaged in a classroom only days later, I would go out of my way to let the student know that I noticed their engagement and success. I observed slight self-control improvement, but the student was immediately aware that they were demonstrating good self-control.

I would use low-profile interactions with the students who were improving in the large classroom setting. Students appeared appreciative of my brief and quiet words of congratulations. On other occasions, I would ask for the student agenda book. In it, I would write a note to the student's parents, something like: "Leon did a great job in class today! He helped problem-solve a math assignment with his peers during the group activity. I was proud of him today, and I thought you should know!"

Keep things simple by pointing out and praising the good things and the changes you see. In this way, the student learns that they are capable of self-control.

Weigh Your Responses

We must realize that youth will listen to our advice, and some may follow through on the recommendation. Take care in the way you help them solve a problem, and evaluate your clarity in the message.

As a youth, I sometimes followed through on the advice given.

In my mind, it was a perfect day. I was enjoying my friends at the community center. We were all elementary school-age youth on summer break. We had lots of energy and ideas about how to engage in fun. There was no thought about school, and those summer days seemed to go on forever. As I recall, the only thing on my mind was playing and socializing.

My favorite games at the community center included softball, kickball, and board games. Occasionally, we would do art projects. With all the fun, I never expected to get a bloody nose from a bully's sucker punch.

The community center supervisor's responsibilities included mowing the grass in the community center. On my bloody-nose day, while he was cutting grass, I played with a few other youths. I don't remember all the details, but another kid and I became involved in a verbal conflict. He was trying to intimidate me verbally. Because of our age, neither of us had effective communication skills for dealing with disputes. Out of nowhere, he punched me in the nose. The bully caught me off guard.

With my bleeding nose, I was not sure what to do. Teachers had insisted that physical conflict was unacceptable. I didn't immediately respond to the bully's punch. I saw the community center supervisor riding the lawn mower, so I asked him for some advice.

He was busy mowing and didn't seem overly concerned about my bloody nose. Without turning the mower off, he listened to my short story about being punched. I told him about the bullying and my confusion about handling the situation. He yelled over the mower noise to punch him in the nose. After providing his advice, he quickly put the mower back in gear and drove away.

He had given me a clear directive for solving the problem. I walked to the bully and punched him in the nose. My actions ended the bullying. However, many other consequences could have transpired from my punch.

For the rest of the summer, the bully and I got along well. We never became great friends, but there was no more bullying.

Since those summer days as a youth, I have had what feels like thousands of conflicts with people. Some of those people were bullies. Self-control to avoid physical conflict is a much better strategy than physical conflict. It's much better to learn nonphysical strategies to deal with disputes.

I bring up the story of my bloody nose because, like many of your mentees, I was searching for answers as a young person and went to an adult and asked for advice. Your mentee may also request your advice. When they ask, you should think carefully about your response.

You will often hear adults share that kids don't listen. This is only sometimes the case. "Punch him in the nose" is straightforward advice. Still, any reasonable person would see that if that is the only strategy you use, it will eventually get you into a lot of trouble.

I have met students who have authorization from a parent to fight with any person who might be displaying disrespect. This isn't a good formula for success, but when I met with the parents, they reinforced the strategy of only one option—fight. The parents were looking at life differently than I. The outcome would not be a success.

Although it's crucial to keep things simple, be strategic and precise with advice that might help a mentee in current and future situations. Teach your mentee the principles of success.

Chapter 16

Patience

B e patient with your mentee. Many youths struggle with self-control. It takes time to learn effective self-control. Value systems and
experiences directly affect self-control effectiveness. If a value system
rewards poor self-control behaviors, your mentee may have challenges
learning new concepts about self-control.

Young people are different. Each one is unique. For example, youth
have different levels of respect for others. Some have a value system
where respect is essential for learning. For others, respecting others may
not be as important.

For decades I have trained in martial arts and practiced with hundreds of people to learn the skills of self-defense. This practice was a
great way to meet and learn more about people. It's interesting how
what I learned about people participating in self-defense paralleled my
real-world experiences outside of martial arts training facilities. I was
able to observe self-control and lack of self-control.

Self-control during sparring and physical contact requires awareness
of safety. Martial arts practitioners don't like to be injured by someone
being careless.

Most people who train in self-defense know there is always a chance of
injury. It's a contact sport, after all. But injury isn't the objective of practicing

with others. I was not interested in participating in any martial arts training facility where injuring your training partners was acceptable.

If you injure your training partners, they will not want to train with you.

Learning Pursuit Pointer #16

Those who show respect usually get respect in return.

A majority of martial arts training facilities are not training professional fighters. Like most professional athletes, professional fighters accept the high risk of injuries. Even in training facilities with professional martial arts fighters, respect for others is critical. Respect and safety should always be a goal while learning self-defense. Self-control is a part of this process.

Self-control and respect for others are just as crucial in the real world. When we work with youth, we need to watch interactions and then teach patiently. Our goal should be to teach principles relating to the respect of others. Those who show respect usually get respect in return.

White Belts

I found that most white belts (new students) started training with a good amount of respect for others. They came to the training facilities with this respect for others. They didn't have an ego that was out of control. They listened closely to the rules and expectations to avoid getting hurt or hurting others. Unfortunately, those white belts still could injure you. They didn't have a skill level that allowed precise movements while working with partners.

Joint locks are an example of where precision, experience, and body awareness are required to avoid injuries. It takes practice and time to apply joint locks effectively. You can feel the technique working without injuring your partner if you apply just enough pressure. While using joint locks, if you move too quickly or put too much leverage on the joint, your partner is at risk of injury.

Similarly, young people need time to learn self-control. You, as a mentor, may be the first to emphasize how important it is to have self-control in this world.

Many of the respectful white belts I worked with didn't yet have the skill to avoid going too far. They would make mistakes. Their partners left the training facility sore. I once had to go to the hospital for X-rays because of an overzealous beginner. Respect and low skill level due to lack of experience can cause problems.

Low Skill

You might find mentees like the white belts who respected others but were learning new self-control skills. We need to be patient with these people. They have good intentions and care about others, and they're just making novice mistakes. We have an opportunity to help by teaching and providing experience opportunities.

Mentees need our guidance. Point out the problems and mistakes. Just because they may not have demonstrated effective self-control behaviors, we should not take the mistakes personally or give up. By sticking with them, they will learn the skills and experience of someone who has patience and endurance. Demonstrating patience is critical with mentees who have witnessed others give up on them in the past. When you don't give up, you'll develop a trusting relationship.

Training with people who respected others but lacked the skill was always rewarding. These people would usually improve and learn.

However, I also trained new students who didn't come in with the same value system or concern for others. There were white belts who did not seem to value training partners. The reckless new students seemed to have behavioral characteristics that led to these aspects of poor self-control:

- Nervousness

- Lack of awareness

- Disregard for expectations

- Desire to impress others

- Self-focus (ego)

- Low respect for others

We can change some behaviors. Some behaviors are more severe than others. When you work with youth, you'll find a similar pattern. Some of the behaviors will have priority over others.

Teaching Strategies for Low Respect

As mentors, if you have a mentee who seems to lack self-control and respect for others, the following strategies might help in the teaching process:

- Effectively monitor behaviors with others.

- Listen and observe—Why are they struggling with self-control?

- Teach and reteach expectations.

- At the start of each mentoring experience, clarify expectations.

- Consider getting the help of others with specific skills and experiences.

- Identify problems and areas to be improved.

- Engage other skilled instructors in the teaching process.

Even with the teaching interventions, some students might struggle to change their poor self-control behaviors, which can sometimes be unsafe. It may be hard to be patient with mentees who are not safe. I've had a few experiences with these types.

At the martial arts training facility, I sustained injuries from training partners lacking discipline, such as a head wound from a headbutt and a hyperextended elbow from an excessively applied armbar.

As an instructor, I practice patience with students, but I'm firm when it comes to enforcing safety rules. Ignoring self-control problems doesn't help the person who lacks self-control.

Unfortunately, even with patience, students with low self-discipline don't train in martial arts for long because they usually don't like my expectations. As an instructor, I always explain why self-control is necessary, but I never lower my expectations when dealing with self-control.

People are different and come with different values. Mentors must be patient but have high expectations. Like the self-defense instructor, identify why the student struggles with self-control.

Chapter 17

Fact-Finding

Ronald was a young man who needed a mentor and needed to learn fact-finding skills. I was lucky enough to become his mentor.

Within the first month of starting school, Ronald began to have problems dealing with teachers and students. His interactions always seemed to escalate, and he needed to gain better people skills. Because of his behavior, a teacher referred him to me as an intervention.

Ronald's emotions would get the best of him. He couldn't seem to regulate his feelings and would overreact to simple situations. For example, when teachers called on him to answer a question during class, he would think he was unfairly being called out. He would get angry at the teacher and sometimes leave the classroom.

When he had conflicts with others, it never escalated to fighting or physical contact. Instead, he would withdraw and walk away. I observed his overreactions, impulsive responses, and misinterpretation of social cues. Ronald and I developed a good relationship, both recognizing that his social interaction challenges wouldn't help him be successful.

Ronald was passionate about comic book characters. I was not, but since he was, I learned about his favorites. Our discussions about superheroes was another positive aspect of the relationship. He loved telling me about the most recent action adventure.

Ronald and I had to start fact-finding.

After Ronald had outbursts and calmed down afterward, he began to understand that his outbursts weren't beneficial. We needed to find a solution and would brainstorm ideas for strategies on how to deal with this.

Although I shared my expectations, I listened intently to try to find out from him why he was having emotional regulation problems. He grew to trust me because I would listen closely to his perspective.

Ronald eventually started to evaluate himself. He would come to my office, and we would discuss the facts, the successes, and the failures. He would come up with solutions to solve his misinterpretations and impulsive responses. I respected his continual efforts to improve.

Ronald and I found that fact-finding took a lot of time and work, and eventually we were able to celebrate his successes. Ronald had found ways to deal with his spontaneous emotions. He also looked at situations differently as he learned to navigate his interactions with others. I was incredibly proud of his accomplishments.

Observe

When you observe young people in public, how they interact with others can sometimes provide information about self-control skill levels.

Observe your mentee's interactions with adults and peers. A mentee may be very respectful to you; however, while interacting with their peers, you may observe self-control problems: offensive touching, cursing, fighting, and more.

After noting the behavior, share the information in a calm, factual way. Pick someplace private so others are not involved in the conversation. I often ask, "What just happened?" Or I might request for them to tell me what they were doing at the time. Most will be able to share their actions. I then follow up with a question about what they should have done or should be doing. Again, most young people can articulate an answer to this type of question.

Sometimes, young people may not be aware until they hear it from a mentor.

Finally, I'll direct them to replay the behavior appropriately, then I'll comment, "I like your answer. Now do it."

Brainstorm

With your mentee, brainstorm and identify a list of self-control situations that lead to success. This list might serve to identify self-control experiences. Listen while gathering this information. Some mentees with self-control challenges might be very open about a problem. Others might be unable to verbalize difficulties because of their lack of understanding or awareness.

Through the brainstorming activity, the mentor should gain more perspective on how the mentee views self-control.

A youth might report that his grades have been dropping in science class. The first logical question might be this: "Why?"

The youth may share, "I don't like the teacher. He has an attitude." This answer would be an excellent time for your mentee to share more, but you may have to probe with more questions.

"So you feel your teacher might have an attitude. I'm sorry to hear this. What does he do that makes you feel this way?"

The mentee may say, "The teacher doesn't seem fair, and he keeps pushing me."

"What do you mean by pushing you?"

My example conversation demonstrates empathy and a focus on getting information.

Empathy

Showing an emotional connection through the conversation is a way to demonstrate empathy. Show your mentee that you care about the discussion. They'll watch you to notice if you're engaged. Engaged listening might look like the following: verbally confirming feelings but not necessarily agreeing, making eye contact, leaning forward slightly, putting electronic devices to the side, asking sincere questions, and answering your mentee's questions.

Through empathetic discussion, you'll demonstrate that you listen and care. But you'll also need to help by identifying and working with the problem. Keep in mind, empathy doesn't necessarily mean that you agree.

If your mentee trusts you, the conversation should lead to the facts you need. You're gathering facts and acknowledging the feelings of your mentee. Below is an example of the possible fact-finding evidence gathered from a discussion.

Initial discussion evidence:

- Mentee gets poor science grades.

- Mentee doesn't like the teacher.

- Mentee believes the teacher has an attitude.

- The teacher isn't fair.

- The teacher pushes the mentee (verbal pushing).

A deeper discussion reveals:

- The teacher constantly asks, "Why are you not doing your homework?"

- Your mentee isn't doing his homework.

- The teacher shares with your mentee expectations and reason for the homework (pushing).

- Your mentee sometimes talks back to the teacher.

- Your mentee understands that back talk is wrong.

- The teacher is under control and fair when discussing homework.

- Your mentee doesn't feel singled out.

- The teacher praises your mentee when he does well.

- When other students don't complete homework, the teacher responds similarly.

- Your mentee knows that he isn't meeting expectations.

- Your mentee is frustrated with himself.

- Your mentee understands not doing homework has resulted in a falling science grade.

- Your mentee doesn't enjoy doing homework.

- Homework has become a frustrating obstacle.

- Your mentee knows he must take action to improve.

- Your mentee doesn't have a plan for improvement.

- Your mentee needs help from you.

By continuing the discussion, the mentor has a much better chance of identifying problems and opportunities. The initial conversation might not have provided enough information to problem-solve; but by digging further into the topic and gathering evidence, a self-control problem becomes evident.

Facilitate Self-Evaluation

The mentee had an emotional perspective, but after looking closer (self-evaluation), even the youth became aware of the problem: he was not doing his homework.

Not doing homework is an example of a self-control problem. Students must set aside time to do their homework. It's much more fun not to do your homework and instead enjoy fun activities like playing computer games or going outside to play with friends. However, there are consequences for this type of lack of self-control.

Even though computer games might be much more fun than homework, the results and consequences of not demonstrating self-control are not enjoyable. The youth doesn't like getting poor grades, nor does he like having discussions with the teacher about the homework problem. Awareness of the problem can lead to identifying solutions. The mentee may need guidance in identifying ways to improve self-control with homework. This may require additional brainstorming.

The self-evaluation process allows the young person to focus on awareness skills, evaluating themselves rather than constantly looking at outside stimuli. Self-evaluation facilitates an understanding of actions that lead to success.

Generate Solutions

For many mentors, it may feel easier to be direct. Being direct may work with some students but not all. Why get into the additional conversation? The mentor knows the solution. Directness isn't working.

Ask your mentee how they think they can solve the problem. What do they think might be a solution? From the discussion, generate a list of actions. This problem-solving activity, which requires the mentee to identify actions and possibly change habits, will be much more beneficial than another adult giving a directive or recommendation.

You and your mentee would likely generate solutions for self-control issues, similar to the examples below:

- While doing homework, get up and move every ten minutes. After a minute or two of movement, continue with the task.

- After completing homework, enjoy the reward of playing a game or doing something else that is enjoyable.

- When working on homework, avoid triggers (distractions) that lead to not completing assigned work. For example, sitting in front of a computer game, watching friends play outside, sitting in a noisy area of the home, and constantly checking social media might be triggers for some youth.

- When the overwhelming feeling of despair happens, take five deep breaths and visualize yourself feeling confident and happy after completing your homework.

Good job with the list! Now write these on sticky notes and put them in your study area.

Just like adults, when youth help to generate solutions, their opinions may guide them to success. If you provide all the ideas, they won't own those actions to success. When they own their ideas and their actions to succeed, it's much more rewarding when they do succeed.

In my experience of helping students see the benefits of doing homework, I have also found that sometimes not completing homework starts in the classroom. Some students don't have note-taking skills. Effective note-taking helps a student who is struggling with independent study skills.

Others have self-control issues of not listening during class; this behavior leads to a student not understanding concepts needed during homework completion.

The most crucial part of solving the problem is to let your mentee develop ideas and actions. They will own the actions, win or lose.

Youth will often ask for advice during the process of brainstorming. When this happens, it's appropriate for the mentor to provide a good recommendation or provide hints that will allow the mentee to continue the process of identifying actions.

I recommend having your mentee write the actions needed to solve the problem. Everyone stands a better chance of accomplishing objectives if they write their goals.

Celebrate Success

After a plan is in place, identify a time to check progress. If successful, that's the time to celebrate. If it isn't, a youth might have to adjust the plan. Adjustments are normal.

Learning Pursuit Pointer #17

Small successes will provide a framework of how self-control can lead to positive results.

Small successes will provide a framework of how self-control can lead to positive results. Mentees feel more engaged in self-control or any other skill when they have participated in solving the problem. When the mentee provides the ideas, they have much more buy-in than when someone else identifies the solution.

Celebrate success when the actions become a habit—when they complete homework consistently and their grades improve, for example. At that point, your mentee is demonstrating self-control and problem-solving, which is truly a time to celebrate. Think of how gratifying it would be to see your mentee improve by implementing a problem-solving strategy. Fact-finding is a skill to help a young person improve self-control.

Chapter 18

Values and Self-Control

A t one point in my career, I had the opportunity to interview prisoners at a correctional facility. Each of the prisoners had long sentences, and they all volunteered for the interviews, each wanting to share their advice with youth to shed light on the harsh realities of choosing a life of crime.

Most of the young people the inmates met had similar value systems to the inmates. The young people were also living out value-based behaviors that a reasonable person would consider out of control.

My interviews with inmates Henry, Clarence, and Tom showed how values influence behaviors. As a mentor, I was interested to learn their perspectives on how value systems affect a person's life.

During our discussions, we discussed values and self-control. They firmly believed that the young people they were trying to help needed a positive vision. Young people who met with the inmates in the prison had a distorted vision for the future, or they had no vision at all.

Henry was very serious when he shared his memories of his family. "My family problems were out of hand." He was sure the adults in his life outside of his family had no idea. As a young person, he observed violence, drug and alcohol abuse, theft, and incarceration.

Clarence grew up in poverty. His community had adults who directly affected his value system. He shared angrily, "You need to be observant of who kids hang out with. Who is in their support system? The only people who came to us kids after school were the dope dealers. They would gather us up and take us to the pizza shop. Who do you think we looked up to?"

Tom provided the perspective on how other youth influenced his value system. "We saw people looking up to the jocks, this group or another. We asked ourselves, what do we have to do to get this type of attention?" They got attention by acting out with negative behaviors.

He continued, "When we didn't come to school, it was because we were out partying." Tom was clear in his belief that drug and alcohol abuse can ruin a young person's life. He believed that some of the blame for addiction can be linked back to value systems.

Clarence shared in his closing thoughts, "Society is a mess. I am amazed when young guys come in here and make comments like, I'm sure glad I'm here or I'd be dead."

I applaud inmates like Henry, Clarence, and Tom. They're trying to be proactive in reaching young people before they get caught up in a legal system and become incarcerated. I'm unsure if their intervention strategies work, but I'm certain they see the link between value systems and behavior.

As mentors, awareness of value systems, identification of value-based behaviors, and understanding the root cause of problems will help us help young people.

Find Out the Value System

I've worked with plenty of youth who disliked the school system. Unfortunately, usually they had a parent who had a horrible experience in school. Therefore, the youth observed, listened, and learned from the parent that the system was not good.

Self-control is affected by the values learned. Values are a foundation in a person's life.

Are self-control issues or destructive behaviors exhibited because of values and experiences? I believe both affect behavior and actions.

Learning Pursuit Pointer #18

Awareness of choice is important when dealing with powerful value-based behaviors.

When I became aware of youth who had a negative perspective based on values, I understood more clearly why self-control issues and behaviors conflicted with a school code of conduct. I recommend that mentors learn about a mentee's value system. There will be times when the value system causes self-control issues.

After gaining background knowledge about a young person, I kept my expectations high. A value system might conflict with expectations, but we know self-control leads to success. For this reason, I continued to teach self-control strategies.

Make sure your mentee knows they have some control over their future. No one controls every aspect of the future, but the parts we control have much to do with our choices. Awareness of choice is important when dealing with powerful value-based behaviors.

Identify Value-Based Behaviors

Middle school students are social. They also become very focused on their peers, wanting the attention and acceptance of those around them. Some students think they can get attention by being physical or disrespectful to others. Some take the actions too far and engage in bullying. Kids choose to bully, but others can influence that bullying behavior. I have had many experiences where a student learned to bully from an adult who was a bully.

Bullying is aggressive behavior toward another person over time. I'm not talking about a one-time conflict. Instead, a bully usually chooses their target intentionally. Verbal and physical actions cause alarm to the victim over and over again.

Sometimes a bully learns from a value system and the experiences in the system. The bully may have started as a victim. They then use the behaviors learned to cause other people problems. Bullying might be everywhere in the family, community, or school. It might be acceptable as a learned value in a family where aggressive behaviors occur. Although no family structures are the same, it isn't uncommon for some families to have excessive aggressive physical encounters.

Mentors have a lot of work to teach a different path. Bullying isn't a behavior that leads to long-term success. It simply isn't acceptable.

Bullying is one example of learned behavior from a value system. Mentors must do more than identify a value system. We must also use that information to identify value-based behaviors. We can then intervene to help a young person change negative behaviors.

Find the Root Cause

Self-control problems might be the outcome of a crazy value system. Problem behaviors might be easy to see. But the root cause might be difficult to find. If not identified and dealt with, suppressed value-based behaviors might resurface.

Even if you correct and help your mentee with a self-control problem, the underlying problem could still exist. Below are a few reasons students have demonstrated poor self-control in a school setting:

- Poor relationships with adults in school

- Poor self-esteem

- Peer pressure

- Acting out behaviors observed at home

- Verbal or physical abuse

- Unclear expectations

- No respect for authority

- No positive role models

- Distrust for the school system

- Trauma

When you find out the real reason for the poor behavior, someone other than you might be the person who helps. We can deal with many problems; however, severe issues might need special care. You may need outside assistance. For example, special counselors should handle physical or substance abuse situations.

Although we might not be able to guide our mentees through all situations, we can address many of the problems. Never overlook how important you are to a mentee. One of the inmates I interviewed shared, "Young people will not always take the initiative to build relationships with adults. Adult role models need to take initiative."

Chapter 19

High-Quality Questions

E xceptional problem solvers know the importance of asking high-quality questions. To solve problems, a person needs to be clear about
what they face. What are the specifics of the impending situation?

To be proficient at asking questions and problem-solving using questions, you need to listen with intent. You should not be lazy while listening.
To improve listening skills, we can learn from the focusing skills of a
professional portrait photographer.

Professional portrait photographers specialize in taking photographs of
people. The best portrait photographers consistently capture images of
people that shows the viewer something about the person captured in the
photograph. How do they do this time after time?

Find a professional portrait and look closely at the image. Are the eyes in
focus? In most cases, portrait photographers focus intently on the person's
eyes. If the eyes of the model are out of focus, the portrait is most likely
worthless.

> **Learning Pursuit Pointer #19**
>
> *People who are exceptional problem solvers know the importance of asking high-quality questions.*

Listen with Intent

When we listen, the focus of our attention should be the person who is speaking. Look at their eyes. What do they say? Just like a professional photographer, you may find a variety of feelings coming from a person's eyes: intensity, boredom, emotional distress, happiness, restlessness, and many more types of emotions. Why is the person showing these types of feelings? Good listeners should be able to include questions linked to emotions. Without observing the eyes, you might miss opportunities to ask a practical question based on emotion.

Adjust the Conversation

A professional photographer rarely begins taking a portrait without some positioning of the subject. Posing a person requires an understanding of how the body's positioning will look in a still photograph. The photographer has control of the situation and will offer suggestions. However, professional photographers know there are times to back off and let the model take over. That awareness makes all the difference in the world with the photograph.

Like posing a portrait subject, a good listener makes conversational adjustments. They strive to find out more by looking at a person's eyes and taking cues from their posture. How are they sitting or standing? Are their arms crossed? If so, are they stressed out, or is it cold in the room?

Once I was having a conversation with someone sitting in front of a table. As we were having the conversation, the person put her head down on the table. This told me a lot about her emotional state of mind: she was overwhelmed. The conversation continued, but I was very strategic. I didn't want to put her into more duress, and I also didn't leave her.

One of the most significant differences between a professional photographer and an amateur photographer is how much they understand and use light. The professional photographer controls lighting. Many amateurs don't see the light on the subject and how it affects the outcome.

The best listeners use questioning to facilitate complete understanding. Without understanding how questions can be used to gain perspective, the listener and speaker's situation is similar to not having a photography lighting plan. Questions don't have to be written down and read; instead, the person needs to know how to offer questions based on specific responses from another person. By listening well and asking good questions, you can grow your problem-solving skills.

After focused listening, a person might think that the conversation is complete. Yes, the person might know you're a caring listener, but it isn't the end of the communication process. The questions might have been fluid and based on experiences in problem-solving, but the conversation may need more. You need to be able to share your views.

Great portrait photographers have a keen sense of when to take a photograph. Because of their visual attention, they know when to activate the shutter release and take the photo.

Just like the portrait photographer, we need to take action at the appropriate times. Sometimes the person talking may be asking for advice. At that time, share your perspective (take a photo). If they never asked for advice, we still need to reflect and communicate our perspectives and thoughts. If you don't share, that could be perceived as agreement with the person, even though you may disagree or have feedback to help.

You may also need to close the conversation with expectations for the future. If you know this is an area of growth for you, you must learn to share information.

Like professional portrait photographers, good listeners focus on their subject. They get rid of the clutter, which might interfere with understanding. They know they need to actively listen. Communication is a moving process that requires awareness. Using questions as a problem-solving tool will only be effective if you listen.

Avoid Single-Response Questions

Developing questions is a special skill for the problem solver. The best problem solvers know how to use and develop questions so they get the information they need.

You can break questioning down into complex situations, but keep it simple for the mentee. Teach your mentee that there are two fundamental types of questions.

First, single-response questions gather one-word or short answers. For example, someone can respond to a single-response question by answering yes or no. They also might be able to answer true or false. Youth are familiar with these types of questions because many of their classroom assessments ask for a simple response.

I hope you will demonstrate single-response questions for your mentee. These questions will generate information that may be enough to take action. They also can lead to more complex questions. Below are a few examples.

Question: "Are you cold?"

Response: "No."

Questioner's Action: No action is required.

Question: "Do you want another dip of ice cream?"

Response: "Yes, please!"

Questioner's Action: Give them another dip of ice cream.

Question: "What is two plus two?"

Response: "Four."

Questioner's Response: "Nice job!"

As a teacher supervisor, I wanted to see more than single-response types of questions. I wanted teachers to provide students with an opportunity to expand their answers. Single-response answers give the questioner information, but teachers need more to assess learning. Judging the level of understanding with a one-word reply may be challenging. Problem solvers may need more information to decide, so they need to understand how to formulate questions that provide more information.

Why are single-response answers not sufficient? If a person only asks questions that provide a yes or no or a one-word answer, they may not be gathering enough information to understand the big picture. For complex problems, this type of questioning won't work.

Consider the scenario where a young person talks to a friend about a math grade. Her friend received a failing grade on a math test. She wants to be a good friend and help. To do this, she offers questions to guide her friend to better math outcomes. Below are a few questions that provide an example of single-response answers.

Question: "What grade did you get on the math test?"

Answer: "F."

Question: "When did you take the test?"

Answer: "Yesterday."

Question: "How many questions were on the test?"

Answer: "Twenty."

Question: "How many did you get wrong?"

Answer: "Ten."

Question: "Did you study?"

Answer: "No."

Question: "Are you going to study for the next test?"

Answer: "Yes."

Questioner's Response: "I know you can do better! Try harder next time! I like that you're going to study for the test next time."

We've gained a small amount of information from the questions and answers above. The student confirms that they can do better, but is there additional information that might help a friend help another friend? Could a failing test grade result from more than not studying? What if a better set of questions had uncovered additional facts? With other evidence, the friend can assist more effectively.

A reluctant-to-talk friend might need open-ended questions.

Use Open-Ended Questions

Open-ended questions allow a person to expand on their thoughts when responding. By expanding on an idea, the listener will have a better understanding. At the same time, the person speaking gains an opportunity to talk about a concept. They might even talk themselves into a solution.

Whenever a person has to answer specific questions, they have an opportunity to provide details. Top-notch problem solvers might routinely ask the right questions. In contrast, others need help finding solutions because they need help organizing their thinking. Teaching our mentees how to ask questions gives them a better chance of getting a clear understanding and improving their listening skills. In addition, it may help them solve problems by asking themselves questions.

Here's an example of a conversation between two friends, where one friend tried to advise about how the other could raise their grades. The questions are simple but allow for open-ended responses.

The conversation started with a friendly discussion that revealed "I didn't do very well on a math test. I'm not very happy."

Question: "What grade did you get on the test?"

Answer: "F."

Questioner's Response: "You must feel horrible about the grade. Are you okay?"

Answer: "I guess. It'll be okay."

Question: "When did you take the test?"

Answer: "Yesterday."

Questioner's Response: "I remember now. You told me you were going to be busy studying over the weekend."

Question: "Were the questions on the test what you expected?"

Answer: "Not really."

Open-Ended Question: "What type of questions were on the test?"

Answer: "The teacher had ten true and false questions, five short-answer questions, and five open-ended questions."

Open-Ended Question: "Wow! How did you get ready for that type of test?"

Answer: "I tried to study over the weekend, but I got caught up in watching some shows."

Questioner's Response: "I can tell you're not happy about this. What did your teacher say?"

Answer: "He said that he was disappointed. He did share that he would allow us to work on the problems we missed for some partial credit. I need to get busy and start studying."

Open-Ended Question: "How are you going to study? Do you have a plan?"

Answer: "I still need to figure that out, but I know I need to take advantage of the opportunity."

Question: "When do you have some free time? Are you interested in studying with a friend?"

Answer: "I could study tomorrow night after field hockey. Are you interested in stopping by? Reviewing my notes and preparing for the upcoming retake should take about forty-five minutes."

Questioner's Response: "Absolutely! That works for me. Let's plan on it."

The friend didn't utilize fancy communication tricks. They were empathetic and authentic, wanting to help but needing to collect more information in order to learn more about the problem. By including open-ended response opportunities, they offered help and even became a study partner.

Open-ended questions don't have to be formal (preplanned and written). Instead, questions will naturally follow answers. Consciously thinking about how you phrase a question will help you gather the information you need during the problem-solving process.

None of the questions would have made a difference without empathy and good listening skills. The questioner got the information needed to help a friend and demonstrated caring as they asked the right questions. Not everybody knows how to use open-ended questions, but most problem solvers learned that they need more information than some people will share. Learning how to use open-ended questions is a way of demonstrating self-control. If you can strategically solve more problems by asking questions, you can control outcomes better.

Memorize Eight Words

Some people seem to naturally know when and how to ask questions to gain more information. They don't have to think about the questioning process strategically. Others might benefit from using question starters.

There are eight words a person could use in the questioning process to move from simple response questions to open-ended questions: *when, where, who, how, would, can, why,* and *what.* Finding a way to remember these words helps in the questioning process. They are not the only words that help in questioning, but they will be handy if your mentee needs to remember how to start questioning.

How can you memorize the words? Some people have no problems remembering words, facts, dates, processes, and other memorization activities. For others, it's much more challenging. One strategy you and your mentee might find helpful is organizing the eight words into a story. I recommend you make the story animated and exaggerated so you'll better remember the story and sequence of events. By using a story format as your memorization technique, the question starters will probably remain in your mind better than simply trying to remember the words on their own.

Below is my animated story. It may not make sense to others, but that's okay. It's meant just for me, to help me remember the words.

When I was daydreaming yesterday (when), I thought about a trip to the zoo (where). While walking through the zoo, I heard a loud "hooooo" (who) sound. I looked up and saw a giant metal owl. The owl was not alone. Sitting beside the owl was a huge wolf made of glass. When the wolf saw me, it began howling (how). The owl and wolf were seated on wood (would) painted purple and yellow. Underneath the wood was a six-foot-diameter tuna fish can (can), and underneath the can was a speaker system shaped like a *y* (why). The word *why* was booming continuously over the speaker. Each time the word *why* was broadcast through the speaker system, the wood, can, and *y* structure lit up with lights. Each light was at least a 100-watt (what) bulb. It was a bright day at the zoo!

While working with young people, I could share my story, but I want them to make up their own. Their stories should be animated and fun. With exaggerated animation, they'll have a better chance of remembering the story and recalling the eight words used to start questions.

For single-response questions, the words *when*, *where*, and *who* are great question starters. It may be more challenging to use these three words to engage someone in an open-ended response. However, they can provide some simple facts about any situation. Without these three pieces of information, it might be hard to get to the big picture.

The open-ended questions can be presented more easily by recalling the question starters *how, would, can, why,* and *what.*

Problem solvers improve control over their environment by asking questions. Asking the right questions provides opportunities for greater understanding. By teaching your mentee how to ask questions, you're teaching them how to be problem solvers.

Chapter 20

Organizational Strategies

O ur goal as mentors should be to help our mentees see chaos and fix the chaos problem with organizational strategies. In a young person's world, chaos usually doesn't look like chaos found in a military event or social unrest. It could be as simple as opening their book bag or locker and looking. Unorganized book bags are much easier to fix than a revolution.

I took the job as a high school principal during the summer. Students were not on campus, but it was a hectic time. As with all school principals, a priority in my job was working with people. Parents, teachers, organizational leaders, district administrators, and students wanted to talk. I met with anyone who requested a meeting.

In those meetings, people shared their concerns, each one identifying problems. I had to categorize the issues. One of the ways I categorized was to determine who was sending me the problem: my boss, parents, teachers, students, or others. Categorizing allowed me to think logically about assisting and solving the problem.

There was a theme among parents and teachers. Both groups felt strongly that cutting school was a problem. During the school day, large numbers of students got into cars and exited the school property. Since I was new and never in the building to observe student transitions, I had to gather evidence about the problem.

The offending students came to school and participated in morning classes. However, they didn't show up to classes scheduled at the end of the day. Were they tired? Could they only take half a day of high school? What was driving them out of the building at noon? I needed evidence to answer the questions.

We organized the evidence by looking at systems. School class schedules, attendance reports, school procedures, and discipline referrals for cutting school were all a part of the system. It took little time to identify a problem.

The schedule included lunch. In the minds of many of our students, socializing with friends at lunch on campus was more fun than going to class. Furthermore, other students enjoyed socializing and picking the meeting location off campus.

We created a list of facts associated with the problem:

- Most cutters (students who didn't go to class or an assigned area) walked to their cars and left the school grounds at lunch.

- No one was actively trying to stop this mass student exit.

- At the same time, there was an open lunch procedure, which caused an inside-of-the-school supervision problem.

- With open lunch, students could go wherever they wanted to go during lunch. Roughly 10 percent of the students wandered throughout the school, some taking their lunch into the hallways or classrooms to eat.

- Students utilized their free time to wander the hallways unsupervised.

- For the teachers and administrators, supervising the chaos inside was a priority. They didn't have time to focus on students leaving school.

- The cutters who had cars and wanted to leave school to socialize took advantage of the easy opportunity to go.

By organizing information, we were able to identify the problem. I shared the information with the people concerned. I also decided there would be no more unsupervised lunch activities. During lunch, students were to report to the cafeteria.

We used the end of the summer break to develop a plan and a timeline, and we shared the new procedure with teachers, students, and parents.

Organizational strategies helped us identify the problem: the system and procedures facilitated the chaos and safety concerns. I was lucky to have a team to help solve the problem. Without a clear perspective of the situation, we might not have been able to improve.

Categorize

Book bags can tell a story about a young person's organizational skills. If a young person can't secure items quickly from a bag, there might be a problem. As mentors, we have a great opportunity to teach organization skills through categorizing—strategies that can be duplicated over and over from youth to adulthood.

One way to categorize is to organize notebooks by subject. Youth should be able to access handouts and important papers easily. Notes within the notebooks should be secured in a designated area.

To categorize, have the youth separate items into similar units or subjects. Open up the notebooks and see if they show order by category: lecture notes, homework assignments, project plans, exam preparation, research notes, concept maps and diagrams, personal reflections, and reference materials.

The young person should have some sequence or way to identify parts of the notebook. Categorizing will help them find important paperwork.

Systemize

After categorizing, young people should learn how to systemize. What are the systems involved in keeping an organized book bag?

The purpose of a school book bag is to secure important documents and materials to assist in learning. When a student systemizes the organization of the school book bag, they need to think of important connections to consistently having a book bag ready to go. Here are a few examples of book bag systems at work:

- Preparing the book bag for the next day

- Securing the book bag in a specific location at the end of the day for easy access in the morning

- Weekly checks to reorganize and resupply resources such as pencils, paper, and batteries

- Having a process in place to always have the book bag when needed

Learning the systems associated with a book bag will give a young person a critical perspective. Systems are all around us, and we become more effective organizers when we become aware of systems.

Learning Pursuit Pointer #20

Systems are all around us, and we become more effective organizers when we become aware of systems.

Lists

Functional lists will support an organizational system. Young people should learn the significant benefits of applying a list to help in the book bag organizational process.

Youth will find lists helpful in problem-solving, but they can also use them proactively to avoid problems.

As you work with your mentee on organizational strategies, you can have them create a list of opportunities and problems associated with their book bag. This list type can help them understand why book bag organizational strategies are beneficial.

Simply put, a list might help young people identify what's in a book bag. This list will be invaluable as a reference when they're packing a book bag, helping ensure all resources are packed and ready for the day.

Additionally, a young person could use a list to identify actions for success. When people deal with change—like becoming more organized—a simple list of what to do can help. For example, an actionable list for end-of-day preparation might include the following:

- Secure homework in the appropriate categorized section of the notebook.

- Place notebooks in the book bag.

- Check to make sure resources like pencils and paper are in the book bag.

- Move the book bag to the front door for easy pickup in the morning.

- Review the book bag item list to ensure all items are in the book bag.

Like the other components of organizational strategies, learning how to create a list will help a young person be successful as they learn how to organize.

Check on Progress

You might also include a deadline for when the book bag organization skills will be in place. This may take time and checks by an adult, but the scheduled inspections will help us evaluate the effectiveness of the new strategy.

Youth may have questions and request feedback as they try to build organizational skills into their lives. The scheduled check-ins are a perfect time to answer questions and adjust as necessary.

Once the process becomes a habit, inspections may no longer be needed. Organizing a book bag is just one example of a process that can become a life skill for a young person. After they master the book bag, move on to the messy room. Organizational strategies can help!

Chapter 21

Proactive Organizing

W hile teaching manufacturing and entrepreneurial skills to high school students, proactively organizing their ideas was essential to their learning. None of the students in my class had a business or worked a manufacturing job, so they needed ways to organize their business ideas.

I assigned the students to cooperative groups. This type of grouping requires students to take on specific roles and responsibilities. Each group needed a leader. They developed résumés to find the most qualified leader and fill other important positions within the company.

Most of the students needed to gain experience in writing a résumé. The organizational strategy of outlining was helpful as they wrote résumés.

Keaton, a student in the class, was a natural leader on the football team, and his résumé highlighted his athletic accomplishments and other experiences. I wasn't surprised when his group selected him as the chief executive officer.

Keaton understood football, a solid team sport, and, therefore, he made every effort to get his group to function like a team. He used graphic organizers to get his classmates talking and to start accomplishing his objective of building a team.

Keaton was interested in facilitating discussions about the organization's mission, and he wanted all members of the group to participate. The team used a graphic web to brainstorm ideas about purpose, core values, target audience, products, and services. The outcome of the graphic web work was a mission statement.

After developing a mission statement, he used flowcharts to clarify responsibilities. Using this type of graphic organizer, each team member knew their purpose and responsibilities.

Paperwork began to pile up. All business leaders can relate to the paperwork craziness in a business. Keaton observed this organizational challenge and did an excellent job of tackling the challenge head-on. He and his team labeled folders and organized them for easy access.

Keaton's team became proficient at using proactive organizing strategies and resources. The team had great success in the production of the school promotional product. More importantly, however, they learned how to organize.

Learning Pursuit Pointer #21

With organizational skills, life becomes more manageable, with enhanced effectiveness and efficiency.

With organizational skills, life becomes more manageable, with enhanced effectiveness and efficiency. Essential resources become easily accessed. Teach your mentee the power of organization by sharing a diverse toolkit of proactive organizational resources: graphic organizers, outlines, spreadsheets, labeled folders, alphabetical sorting, item grouping, subject categorization, color coding, online organizers, chronological organization, and the use of Post-it® Notes.

Graphic Organizers

Graphic organizers are wonderful categorizing tools used to organize information. There are many types of graphic organizers—Venn diagrams, timelines, facts versus opinions, flowcharts, idea funnels, thought webs,

KWL charts (What do you **know**? What do you **want** to know? What have you **learned**?)—many youths have likely encountered in the classroom. These tools have value well beyond the classroom as well.

When school teams have to review large amounts of data, categorizing helps show patterns or characteristics. Information sorting improves understanding. Drawing a line down a flip chart paper to organize ideas is a simple example of a graphical way of organizing. On one side, we might identify a problem or evidence. On the other side, we could document possible solutions.

Graphic organizers can be simple. When youth know they can solve problems by categorizing using a graphic organizer, they're one step closer to being more productive.

Outlines

Outlines are another excellent tool for organizing thoughts. Writers use outlines to summarize and organize topics. When categorized, they can expand on the information and show connections.

Outlines can be created individually or with others in a small group, and they're a great way to generate ideas. The ideas don't have to be highly detailed. Instead, the crucial points will sometimes lead to discussion and a greater understanding. Grouping thoughts and main points helps in the problem-solving process.

Teach your mentee that when using an outline, they don't have to expand upon details on the first draft.

Outlines are also helpful to share with others to generate ideas. Presenters can use an outline format to summarize important concepts. While creating an outline with others, you may generate ideas beyond personal expectations. It's always a positive plan to get additional insight into a problem by talking to others, especially when they're close to the problem.

Spreadsheets

Spreadsheets and databases help organize and consolidate large amounts of information. Many decisions rely on essential details that otherwise would be unusable without some organizational tool.

Spreadsheets help the problem solver, but they first must be aware of how specific spreadsheets work. For example, most spreadsheets allow the user to sort information. Therefore, accurate information makes a spreadsheet valuable. Conversely, insufficient data in a spreadsheet can lead to poor decision-making.

Any chance you get to help your mentee learn about databases as an organizational tool will help them in the future. In leadership positions, young people need to know how to collect and review data to make accurate decisions. With spreadsheet and database skills, they can leverage an essential problem-solving skill.

Julia, a student, has a problem. As a part of Julia's responsibility, she must administer and interpret a student survey. The survey will provide the student-led leadership team with data to identify an environmental project. The leadership team wants student input on what activities in the community are most popular with students at the school.

Once the information is collected, the leadership team will organize and facilitate the project. But first, your mentee has to create a survey and transfer the data into a database or spreadsheet.

From her mentor, Julia understands that the database will help her sort through large amounts of information and help her team.

Julia starts with a free online survey to collect data. Then her principal will advertise the survey link. Julia can see student excitement and participation in real time as the surveys load into the spreadsheet. Julia smiles as she thinks, "This is so much easier than sending paper surveys to each homeroom."

After the deadline of the survey, Julia starts sorting survey information. The spreadsheet identifies the priorities of the students of the building.

She will be able to lead the leadership team discussion at the next meeting with data. Because of her efforts, the team will better understand student interests and be on its way to planning the environmental cleanups in the community.

The online survey was a tool that created a spreadsheet. Teaching your mentee how to use these tools to solve problems or gather information can become a valuable lesson.

Labeling Folders

It may seem like a simple strategy, but you would be amazed at the number of people not using this organizational tool. Labeling folders can make a difference in a person's organizational success. Young people might need to learn about the usefulness of labeling. As mentors, check with your mentees to see if they label folders or other organizational tools.

While working as an educator, I began to collect helpful information about curriculum units. Labeling the folders allowed me to find specific units quickly.

Young people might have different responsibilities and connections with other organizations, but it's never too early to learn the power of organizing folders. Although our world seems to be moving toward organizing electronic files, having a hard copy of an important document never hurts. For example, by labeling folders for their specific subject areas, they will access paperwork given to them by their teachers and have instant access to educational resources.

How does labeling a folder link to self-control? Knowing that you can quickly gather information leads to better use of time. Lost paperwork because of poor filing and organizing equals frustration and stress. People with organizational skills can save energy searching for lost papers. They control the outcome because of personal self-control.

So far, I've mainly discussed physical items (paperwork) going into folders. In today's digital world, effectively labeling electronic folders is just as valuable an organizational process as having physical documents. Like physical documents, email or other electronic data folders can be labeled and organized. If an electronic record is worth saving, it's worth putting that document into a folder. Teach your mentee how to save time using this strategy. They need this life skill.

Should we keep electronic or physical/hard copy documents? Regardless of which you decide, it's important to learn both physical and electronic filing and organizational systems. Some important documents should definitely remain in a physical file. When I need my birth certificate, for example, I go to the folder with a label called "birth certificate."

Let's teach our mentees the labeling strategy now so they are effective organizers both as young people and as adults.

Additional Organizing by Groups and Color Code

After you label your folders, you need to organize those folders. Organize folders by alphabet, color, and various groupings.

Alphabetical organizing is a standard method for organizing information. Some youth will not have large amounts of physical documents that require alphabetical organization. However, the skill of learning to manage items by alphabet will help them in the future.

Without a filing cabinet, a young person can still practice filing. They can put documents into folders and then place those folders into boxes. Storing alphabetized folders in a box is as effective as having a filing cabinet. We need to keep it simple so that they learn the importance of organization.

Color-coding groups or other information is a handy skill, particularly for educators. For example, the school nurse could organize all emergency medical information for students alphabetically, color coded by grade. Use color coding in a way that works best for whatever industry and role you're in.

Online organizational tools allow people to organize large groups of information by category or title. Sorting like this allows a person to organize data to make decisions about various situations. In the school scenario I shared earlier, we could sort through large amounts of evidence using a database that categorizes by discipline, attendance, grades, individualized education plan, and other data.

Your mentee will benefit from learning about data collection and organizing data electronically. Counting by hand—which I used to do, but thankfully don't have to anymore—is extremely time-consuming. Sorting using technology is much more efficient.

Another sound organizational strategy is to create folders in your email program or storage software. Use folders and subfolders to group similar emails or files together, making your searches more streamlined and successful. With this strategy, information becomes easily accessible.

Organizing by Year

Organizing files by year is a fundamental skill that works well for certain file types—tax documents, for example. Although most young people will not have experience filing taxes, adults will be aware of the dreaded tax filing process. A folder with a tax year can allow a person to keep all essential tax documents for the year in one location. This is much easier than sorting through endless piles of paper and is a great organizational skill to teach youth.

Business Contacts, Clubs, and Other Organizations

Many young people are associated with at least one club or team. Ask your mentee if they have a folder for the paperwork from the organization they're associated with and share fundamentals with them of how to keep it organized. Keeping paper from organizations separate and categorized will allow easy access to receipts and other important documents.

Post-it® Notes

Post-it® Notes are great tools. Using them is an excellent way to facilitate ideas and categorize those ideas into workable actions.

Ramon was chair of the student council. Excited to accept the position's responsibilities, he scheduled a meeting with classroom representatives, ready to get work right away.

Twenty young people sat in front of Ramon. It was time to generate ideas on how to improve the cafeteria environment, one of the student council's main initiatives for the year. Ramon was prepared with Post-it® Notes to organize the group's thoughts and categorize possible recommendations for improvement.

Ramon organized the classroom representatives into small groups. The groups were manageable and allowed participants to discuss topics openly. He wanted to hear all voices at the meeting, and small groups facilitated the opportunity for all the students to participate.

Ramon tasked the groups with generating ideas about improving the cafeteria environment. He shared, "Students are not happy with our cafeteria. The student council leadership wants me to get your input and bring back your ideas because your ideas are important to us. After identifying ideas, we plan to categorize those ideas from most important to least important."

The groups received Post-it® Notes, and each participant in the group could present in writing two recommendations. Since there were twenty representatives at the meeting, there were forty recommendations to review and categorize.

Ramon emphasized that each person's ideas were important. However, he couldn't take forty recommendations back to the student council leadership. "Before the end of this meeting, we'll use the ideas written on these notes to determine the most popular ideas," he said. "This will give the leadership team a few of our best ideas."

A hearty discussion ensued. Ramon moved around to each of the groups to monitor the conversations. He also used the opportunity to answer any questions about the process or leadership requests.

After the groups appeared ready to move forward with the next step of the Post-it® planning and categorizing, he organized the Post-it® Notes into categories and practiced a presentation with each group. After the small-group presentations, group leaders presented ideas to all participants at the meeting.

As each small-group leader presented, Ramon and leaders categorized the Post-it® Notes into similar groups, and popular themes began to emerge:

- More selections of healthy snacks

- An improved environment through decorations and paintings

- A layout change that would include round tables in a more casual environment

With the help of Ramon, group presenters did a fantastic job organizing the Post-it® Notes recommendations into categorized themes. Students felt the three big ideas would improve the cafeteria environment. They confirmed their voices were heard and felt comfortable with Ramon returning the three recommendations to the leadership team.

Ramon employed a method of organization that utilized Post-it® Notes. He then presented the suggestions to the leadership team with confidence, backed by the positive results from the group activities. His presentation featured detailed data to support his points.

As we look for ways to engage young people in leadership opportunities, we can brainstorm organizational ideas and strategies for them to use as leaders. Post-it® Notes are great for problem-solving and organization and can come in handy for any meeting facilitator.

Chapter 22

Routines

Young people can benefit from learning effective routines. A routine can be either good or bad. We must teach young people the benefits of routines and how to evaluate them for positive outcomes.

Mrs. Johnson, the senior secretary for our school, came into my office. She was shaking her head. "I need your help. Josh has been late fifteen times this month. He doesn't seem to care!" She pointed in the direction of the lobby, where I saw Josh, seated and waiting.

I didn't know Josh and hadn't had any prior interactions with him. I asked Mrs. Johnson, "Have you had any success reaching his parents?"

She immediately looked frustrated. "I can never reach his parents. I leave messages, and the automated messenger sends a message every day that he's late. We get no response from the family." She started pacing in front of me. "His grades are horrendous. With no response from his parents, I don't see any way to change his behavior. Can you talk to him?"

I rose from my seat and said, "Absolutely. Maybe I can find out why he's late, and we can work on his grades."

Mrs. Johnson and I walked intently out into the lobby. Josh, a sixth-grade student, was slumped in the seat of one of the lobby chairs. He had dark rings under his eyes. "Hi, Dr. Carmack." He clearly wasn't excited about seeing me, but he was polite.

"How are you, Josh?" I noticed he was still slumped in the chair, which I assumed was more from his being tired rather than having poor posture. "I'd like to take a little time to talk to you. I hear you're having some challenges with grades and being late."

"Sure thing, Dr. Carmack." He stood up slowly.

"Do you have a book bag?" I noticed Josh didn't have any books or a book bag. Most students coming to school with book bags that are full of books, homework, and study resources. Josh had nothing.

"No sir. I didn't have any homework." Josh followed me into my office. Mrs. Johnson looked less stressed and seemed to appreciate that I was going to speak to Josh about his lateness.

Once in the office, I pulled up a database that provided information about Josh's academic performance. He wasn't doing well and was failing his first two classes of the day. His other grades were Cs and Ds. "It looks like you're not doing well with your grades. You seem like a smart young man. What's going on?"

Josh paused. "I really don't like school."

"Why?" I asked.

Josh didn't respond. He looked off to the side toward the wall, not making eye contact.

I looked further at his academic and behavioral records. There were no major behavioral issues other than being late to school. He wasn't defiant to teachers and didn't seem disrespectful.

"What do your parents say about your low grades?"

Josh looked at me slowly but again paused. "We don't talk about grades." He immediately glanced over to the wall. He frowned briefly and then went back to staring to avoid eye contact. It was clear he was not interested in talking about this problem.

"How can we help you? Again, you look like you're very capable of getting good grades. You also look like, with effort, you could get to school on time. We want to be able to help you. Talk to me, Josh."

Josh said, "I don't know. I know I should do better."

"You look tired. Tell me about your evening routine. Working with other students, many of them have a routine that doesn't allow them to get enough sleep. What's your routine?"

Josh glanced back at me and made eye contact. He looked genuinely interested. "I like to watch TV." He seemed to be sincere. He sat a little straighter in the chair and appeared interested in talking. He was excited about sharing his hobby.

"How much television do you watch? What shows do you like?"

"I really like old movies, Dr. Carmack. I watch them in the evening. Some of the best movies are on late at night. That's when I watch them."

Josh shared that he had a routine. His routine at night was freedom and watching television. No adults checked to see how he was doing or what he was doing. He had a television in his room and controlled how long he watched it. He shared that he felt guilty about not doing well in school because of his television routine. Hours of television in the evening left no time for schoolwork.

"I know I have a problem watching too much television," he said. "I guess I need to make some changes."

I was happy to see Josh acknowledge the problem: he had a routine that was out of control. Television was almost like an addiction to him. It was easy to sit in front of the television and forget about school or other problems. I was sure we could help Josh change his routine, but I knew it would take time. The positive reveal from our conversation was that he also knew that his routine was a problem.

Involve Others

Josh needed immediate intervention, and I needed to find ways to support him and create a plan to change the routine. Together, we agreed that making Josh part of the planning process would be a priority. He also was able to identify a mentor to help in the planning process, which allowed him to feel like he was also a part of the decision-making process. Josh's buy-in was key. If we had developed a plan for him, he might not have had the same enthusiasm and perspective on improving.

I said to Josh, "Let's create a plan to help you with your evening routine. Do you want anyone special to help?"

He looked happy that this was an option. "That would be great! I like Mrs. Johnson. I think she would be someone who would be able to give me some advice." He smiled and looked out of the office door toward Mrs. Johnson's desk. He must have appreciated that she never gave up on him and didn't lower her expectations. She wanted him to come to school on time and do well academically.

We took the time to bring Mrs. Johnson into the planning process. She was happy to assist.

In most cases, we would have included the parent in the planning process. We invited Josh's parent to the planning meeting, but they chose not to attend.

Mentors need to communicate with parents. You may have ideas about creating plans that will benefit your mentee, but if the parent doesn't buy into the planning process and feel a part of the process, there could be hard feelings. At the very minimum, keep parents informed.

Set Measurable Goals

Another critical aspect of the plan was that the goals were measurable and that the measurements were easy to understand. Vague goals that don't have some measurable outcome are rarely effective. In that case, it would have been easy for Josh to say, "I will improve." What does improvement look like? With our established measurements, we were able to measure progress more precisely. Josh understood that the measurements were necessary.

We allowed Josh to identify his goals for the plan. He wanted to improve academically, and he would be able to measure by class grades.

In addition, he set a goal to change stop arriving late to school. His goal was to be on time 90 percent of the time for the first month of his plan. After that, he felt he would be at school on time 100 percent of the time.

Identify Actions

After we set the goals, we identified actions he would have to take to be successful:

- Josh will complete homework and study before turning on the television.

- Josh will meet weekly with Principal Carmack to review the plan goals and actions.

- Josh will be in bed by 10:00 p.m. with the television off.

- Josh will be at the bus stop ten minutes before pickup.

- Josh identified actions he thought would help his pursuit of better grades and on-time behavior. Principal Carmack would be responsible for the following actions:

  - Principal Carmack will meet with Josh every Friday afternoon to review his grades and attendance. If Principal Carmack isn't available, Mrs. Johnson will review the information with Josh.

  - Principal Carmack will attempt to contact Josh's parents to update them about the plan and Josh's progress.

  - Principal Carmack will reward Josh for improvement with cafeteria snack passes and extra time in the gymnasium during the activity class.

    ○ Mrs. Johnson will reward Josh with lunch in the main office.

Josh's rewards for improvement might seem simplistic. I've created many plans with young people. Most of the time, their rewards for achievement have been simple and inexpensive. In many cases, the team of adults would have suggested something other than the reward suggested by the young person. For example, Josh wanted to have lunch with the person he respected, Mrs. Johnson. Josh came up with the idea, and it was fun for him to socialize with his mentor. Mrs. Johnson had to provide the time.

If Josh had been the only participant in the action steps, he might have felt overwhelmed or less enthusiastic about the plan. Instead, he could see that the plan included other people. Josh didn't feel alone. He knew Principal Carmack and Mrs. Johnson had responsibilities connected to the plan.

Look for Improvement Opportunities

As a mentor or a mentee, it's always a good idea to check your routines to see if they could be improved. One day while bicycling, this advice became clear to me.

Our bicycle group was lucky to have a state park with a well-kept bicycle trail. From the parking area, we would unload bikes and take off. Over the summer, we explored the trails.

The trail started with an asphalt path. The first gravel trail was at an intersection close to the start of the bike path and led to a wilderness adventure, so we always took the asphalt path to transition to the gravel trail. The view was always rewarding. We were in a routine.

We also had a routine coming back from the outer parts of the park. There was a steep and fast hill that was always alluring and fun. This part of the trail diverted us from traveling back to the first gravel trail near the entrance. But one day, I decided to take a different path back.

Toward the end of the summer, I decided to go for a ride alone. I took the usual asphalt path and transitioned to the first gravel trail. It was a typical workout and routine. At the end of the ride, rather than ride the fast hill, I chose to go the opposite way on the path.

The path looked different when I traveled in the opposite direction. The view was that of a new trail. Although I had ridden the trail a few times throughout the summer, taking the reverse perspective on the trail provided a different view.

Hills were opposite. Instead of going up, I was going down. Trees had hidden secrets like algae growths or gaps not seen from the opposite direction. Tree groves looked different from the new vantage point. The horizon resembled a magnificent painting as the sun danced over the brush and through the trees. I saw a patch of pink and yellow flowers near a fallen tree. The forest was alive and new in my eyes.

Although I was on the same path, reversing the ride gave me a different perspective.

Learning Pursuit Pointers #22

Always look for ways to improve your routines. If you have a routine that happens without thinking, you might benefit by evaluating it.

Just like the gravel trail, our routines can become so ingrained that we miss opportunities to look at them from a different point of view.

Always look for ways to improve your routines. If you have a routine that happens without thinking, you might benefit by evaluating it. Tell your mentee about what you learned. Share how routines can become ingrained in our lives. A routine, just like other aspects of our lives, might be ready for change. Take a different perspective to see if your routines or your mentee's routines can become more effective.

The Ongoing Process of Evaluating Routines

Let's look at how to improve our routines.

If you teach a group of students, classroom management routines are essential. If you're aware that you're not highly effective in facilitating classroom management routines, what actions must you take to improve? Classroom management routines are one of the fundamental parts of becoming a successful teacher. Without good classroom management skills, the day will seem long and utterly chaotic. For those who lack skills in this area, student learning will be at risk. Poor classroom management skills force many new teachers to leave the profession early.

Effective classroom management has routines that control students and their behaviors. When classroom management routines are understood, most students behave appropriately and follow the procedures set by the teacher. Many teachers allow the students to help develop those procedures: courtesy, listening, participating, controlling self, being respectful, being responsible, and being safe.

Coming to class might seem like a nonessential example of a routine. However, if this routine isn't established and taught, chaos can follow.

A teacher with no routine of how students should enter the classroom might face problems every day. Without an expectation or routine, things can get out of control quickly. In a case like this, an observer might see the following:

- Students socializing outside of the classroom and not reporting to class

- Students socializing and then wandering in whenever they want

- Students not engaged in any learning inside the classroom

- Daily disruptions as students argue, socialize, fight, and act in other disruptive ways

- A loss of time after class starts because students are not seated and prepared to learn

- Loud, chaotic discussions between the teacher and students

- A teacher who might not be observant of problems

- The teacher constantly de-escalating problems because of their lack of routines

Effective teachers establish routines for how students enter class. In that proactive setting, an observer might see the following:

- The teacher positioned at the doorway, verbally greeting each student

- Students moving directly to their assigned seats after they enter the classroom

- Students arriving on time

- Students not loitering inside or outside the classroom

- Students speaking quietly in the classroom and in the hallways

- Upon arriving, students putting materials and educational resources on their desks

- Students who were not in class the previous day getting the previous day's materials

- Students working on an instructional warm-up activity displayed for them at the front of the classroom

- Students requesting permission to leave their assigned seats

- Instruction beginning on time

There may be many more specific routine activities that a teacher could present to students. A good routine will only work if students understand and buy into the routine. There will be students who will not immediately respond appropriately to a routine, and the teacher must know what to do when this occurs. Setting high expectations and following through to ensure that all students meet expectations is a skill teachers learn.

During college, new teachers learn classroom routines. Learning classroom routines from a textbook is like any other kind of learning. Teachers learn best by participating. Textbook strategies can make classroom management routines look effortless; but when the scenario involves actual students, things change. Teachers may have the best plans and routines, but young students can change it all and require the teacher to adjust.

College advisers assign each college student working toward a teaching license a teacher adviser. The teacher adviser has the responsibility to mentor and teach. They want to ensure that the young college student successfully transitions from college to employment. They teach in the classroom, but that teaching experience is short.

Teachers in training participate in a school setting for several months. Their adviser will provide them with feedback about planning, classroom management, instructional practice, teacher and student interactions, and assessments. College students quickly learn how important it is to implement routines.

In addition to learning from an adviser, education majors are matched with a cooperating teacher they can learn from, a process school administrators and college advisers take seriously. As a principal, I worked closely with college and district office staff to ensure that cooperating teachers were highly effective with the student teachers they mentored. The teachers were able to model best practices in the classroom for their mentees. Cooperating teachers who were chosen to mentor student teachers were those who consistently proved they could get the very best academic achievement results for their students.

Students know when they're dealing with a rookie teacher. Some students like to take advantage of student teachers. If the teacher in training shows any weakness, some students will challenge them and misbehave. Many student teachers immediately learn how frustrating it can be to control challenging students. Classroom routines must be taught, re-taught, and explained with even more clarity than the first couple of times taught.

Through the experience of teaching, a student teacher will learn how important it is to teach routines and have high expectations. The student teaching is invaluable. Teachers learn much more from working in the classroom than they do from textbook learning. Unfortunately, student teaching experiences are short; and their next step in the learning process is right around the corner: looking for employment.

Once an aspiring teacher gets a job, college advisers and cooperative teachers will no longer observe and provide them feedback. To many new teachers, that's a relief; nobody is looking over their shoulder anymore. Routines are the responsibility of the new teacher, and they learn quickly that there's still so much learning to do.

New teachers quickly discover that their best intentions for classroom routines are only sometimes effective. They learn there were blind spots in their practices and their learning. They didn't see uncooperative student responses and behaviors coming. Because of this, they must make adjustments. Successful new teachers continue to learn from others.

New teachers are usually assigned official mentors from the school system. Those mentors are experienced teachers who visit the classroom occasionally and give feedback about routines and other vital aspects of teaching. When I talked to hundreds of new teachers, a majority shared that the assigned mentors have great intentions, but new teachers learn much more from unassigned mentors.

The teacher next door might share excellent information about routines. A teacher participating in a department meeting might not be assigned as a mentor but will become actively involved in helping the new teacher with routines. This type of learning from others is invaluable as the new teacher experiments with classroom routines.

New teachers lucky enough to have good administrative supervisors will also have a good resource for information. Supervisors can share what classroom routines work and what routines don't work. Supervisors can observe practices from the most effective teachers in the building and can pass along that information to new teachers.

New teachers who endure and learn from others can fine-tune routines and become highly effective teachers.

As we work with mentees on routines, we should share examples like the new teacher's experience. Routines change over time. The changes come from learning and searching for a better way to implement the routines.

As a mentor, do you see similarities in how a new teacher establishes classroom routines and how you might have experienced the same type of change over time? As you consider your improvement journey, use the summary below of how an aspiring teacher learns skills:

- Textbook and video instruction

- College teachers and advisers

- Discussions with other college students

- Student teacher experience—working with kids

- Lessons learned from a cooperative teacher

- Employment as a "real" teacher

- Assigned mentors

- Unassigned mentors and colleagues

- Supervisor

New teachers who look for solutions and improvement strategies know they are responsible. If they don't take action, they likely won't see much improvement.

Accept Responsibility — Sheepdog Analogy

A sheepdog handler understands the principle of being accountable for results.

Spectators focus intently on the sheep, sheepdog, and handler. Some spectators stand; others relax in their seats. But all are intently watching.

The sheepdog, Foster Finn, lowers his bristling shoulders as he creeps forward. His black-and-white sheening fur makes him look streamlined and ready to accelerate with ease. Finn's head is extended straight from his shoulders, and he is staring with authority at the herd. You might be terrified if you saw those black predator eyes staring at you. There would be no doubt that the eyes communicate that *you're* the hunted.

During the stalking, Finn effortlessly controls each step taken in the sheep's direction. His nose purposely points directly at the sheep. The dog doesn't charge but moves with precision. The sheep seem to realize that the sheepdog is in control. They've never seen this dog before today. The dog appears to be a predator, but for now, the sheep are still calm. They seem to understand that the dog has a job to do and intends to complete the mission.

As Foster Finn moves forward, the sheep look in the direction of the perceived predator. They lean slightly away from the dog, anticipating and instinctively realizing that the dog could attack. The sheep control their fear but appear cautious. In their minds, the dog is just a little too close. They turn and retreat four or five steps away from the dog and immediately reset their feet and eyes to ensure a quick retreat. Again, their bodies lean slightly away from the dog. The dog continues to move toward the sheep in a controlled manner. The sheep are mesmerized.

Sheepdog handlers competing at sheepdog competitions don't like to see chaos. Chaos looks like sheep wandering away from the herd or moving in the wrong direction. During sheepdog trials, sheepdog handlers understand that to win, controlling the herd is the number one priority. Unaware observers may think that the dog is in charge. The handler, however, is the one in control.

An event for sheepdog handlers calls for precision. Judges at the competition rate a variety of skills. In addition to avoiding chaos, below are some of the required herd-control skills you might see at a sheepdog trial competition:

- The away test requires the handler to move the herd away from the handler's location. This may sound easy, but it's not instinctive for the dog to drive the herd away from the handler. In most cases, dogs move a herd toward the handler.

- The handler must be able to separate the group. This is a controlled separation.

- A skilled handler will be able to move sheep into confined areas. Sheep don't instinctively like restricted areas, so this can be challenging.

- In some competitions, the handlers must separate one sheep from the herd.

If something goes wrong in the competition, sheepdog handlers know it's their mistake. Blame should never go to the sheepdog. If chaos comes to the herd, the sheepdog handler is responsible. Responsibility starts way before the competition. Dogs come with different personalities. Sheepdog handlers train dogs to perform specific actions: drive the herd, lie down, circle the herd, go right, go left, and stay.

Dogs are trained not to charge but to follow directions and move with purpose. The dogs must look fearsome because sheep are not impressed with dogs who lack the look of a predator. Handlers train their dogs to stalk the herd.

Like the new teacher looking for routines to control classroom behavior, the dog handler looks for routines that produce exact results with the sheepdog. They learn from experience what training routines work. Dog handlers find the best routines and methods to train puppies to be sheepdogs. When the puppy doesn't respond appropriately to the training, the handler learns something about the training situation. Handlers don't blame the puppy for the mistakes. Instead, the handler is responsible for improving the training routine to help the puppy become successful.

Just as it is for teachers and handlers, evaluating routines should be an ongoing process for all of us. Teach evaluation processes to mentees. When results are not meeting our expectations, evaluate the associated routine. The person performing the routine is responsible. Fine-tuning and learning from mistakes will be an ongoing process. Whatever the practice, evaluation and improvement should be continuous. We must be like the dog handler, continually adjusting dog training routines to get the sheep to move perfectly as planned.

Routines Worth Examining

You and your mentee have many routines. Are those routines effective? Here are a few routines that might be worth examining for effectiveness:

- Start of the day

- Daily routines

- Get it out, then put it away

- Evening

- Leave it or fix it

- Touch it one time

Getting enough sleep helps us in preparation for a brand-new day. Following a good night of sleep, we can perfect the start-of-the-day routine. As I worked with many young people who were chronically late to school, I found that most late students didn't have effective early morning practices. We sometimes found an easy fix, such as purchasing an alarm clock for a kid. One teacher team made the purchase, and the student was on time—problem solved. Other problems might be more of a challenge.

To identify a morning routine problem, a mentor may need to meet with the mentee's parent. Youth may need help seeing the problem and solutions.

In the morning, I like to review my online calendar to set alarms for reminders of upcoming meetings or times I need to transition from one location to another. A youth might benefit from this type of reminder action.

I also take the time at the start of the day to review my goals for the week. By looking at those goals and my mission statements, I am getting ready for the day. I have a focus and know why I am taking specific actions. I keep my weekly goals in front of me and take the necessary steps to do the most critical tasks. Many young people would benefit from the early day planning with their goals. This will help them deal with the day's clutter of unplanned activities.

You might have a more effective start-of-the-day routine than I. Share it with your mentee. You may be surprised at how much this helps your mentee.

Classroom Routines

If you mentor a student, I recommend that you discuss classroom routines. Do they have a routine of entering the classroom and preparing all learning materials? This should be a regular practice. Even if the teacher doesn't reinforce this behavior, it helps a young person learn how to start a formal event. Adults use this skill to prepare for meetings.

Does your mentee know how to utilize note-taking tools, which will provide them with a study resource? I was always amazed at the number of students who didn't take notes. Many of those students didn't get good grades.

Classroom routines should include a discussion about the use of time. Some teachers could be more effective with instructional time. If your mentee has one of these teachers, the student will improve academically by improving time use. Any time a teacher allows students to work independently, students should use that time effectively working on homework activities or organizing materials for after-school studying.

Get It Out, Then Put It Away

The routine of getting things out and putting them away could happen any time throughout a person's day. Young people may need to learn this skill from a mentor. Does your mentee need to learn this routine? It's easy to see the differences between those who utilize this practice and those who don't. If a young person doesn't learn how to put things away after use, mentors should take the opportunity to teach them.

Consider how your mentee works their hobby. If your mentee likes scrapbooking, for example, they may require a lot of materials to create their project: paper, patterned paper, adhesives, pens, stickers, photographs, scissors, embellishments, albums, page protectors, craft knives, organizers, story theme resources, and more. If your mentee scatters materials on the floor and leaves them there once they're finished, it's chaos. An effective routine is to get materials out and put them away after they finish so they can find materials for the next project.

How can you teach the skill of getting things out and then putting them away? When you get the chance, demonstrate it. After, share how using that skill has helped you.

Evening Routine

Life gets much easier if you use the evening to get ready for the following day. Young people may not know this skill—the great power of preparing for the morning.

I'm the type of person who takes a while to get moving in the morning. I found that picking out clothes in the morning was too much to think about in my glazed-over state. Taking too long to make a decision can cause stress. To get rid of the stress, I started preparing my clothes before going to bed. Ta-da! Life in the morning got a little easier.

Ask your mentee about how they secure books and school materials. Is everything ready to go in the morning? If not, why? All school materials should be prepared and ready to go in the morning, put in their designated place so they can be taken out of the house efficiently. Stress can cause mistakes. If the process is not organized and kids have to collect their things at the last minute, they risk forgetting something essential.

They also risk being late for school.

An evening routine might include preparing food for breakfast. Having food readily available in the morning can increase effectiveness.

Part of my morning routine includes preparing the coffee maker the evening before. When I come into the kitchen the next morning, I pour water into the coffee maker and hit a button. My evening routine makes my morning routine much more enjoyable and helps me avoid spilling coffee grounds everywhere.

Since your mentee might not drink coffee, another example of a morning routine is preparing food for quick access. You might agree that transitioning out the door is more efficient if your evening routine includes preparing meals for lunch. This helped my morning schedule tremendously, and I took this non-fun job to the extreme. On Sunday night, I made five lunches and put the lunches in containers. I moved four of the containers to the freezer. Each evening I transitioned a lunch from the freezer to the refrigerator. You might be able to share better examples of evening routine activities with your mentee.

Leave It or Fix It

What do you do when something breaks down? Do you have a routine of setting the broken item off to the side, or do you fix it? Those who put things off to the side may start a bad routine. I know some people who don't follow up and fix items that need repair. We need to teach our mentees to expect things to break. Repairs are a normal part of life. A good life skill is to fix it as soon as possible. If you don't, you're asking for unnecessary chaos and stress.

Homeownership is a rewarding experience and one of the most significant financial investments many people will make in their lives. Homeowners face constant bills: mortgage payments, taxes, insurance, utility bills, home repair costs, and more. The mortgage payments include a principal payment and an interest payment for the loan—loan institutions love receiving the interest payment. When a person pays the principal fee, they are building home equity. Home equity is the difference between the value of the home and the balance of all liens.

Homeowners are aware that the fair market value of the home includes taking care of the property. In other words, if a homeowner doesn't take care of the property, the property's market value will decrease. To avoid this problem, when things need repair, they need to be fixed as soon as possible.

To examine the benefits of a fix-it routine, let's look at two homeowners, Yvette and Sam, and their house maintenance practices. Ten years ago, both homeowners purchased homes for $200,000. They each paid off 50 percent of the purchase price during those ten years, so the outstanding balance of the lien is $100,000.

Yvette had maintained her property well. When a problem occurred and a repair was needed, she took care of it. Over the last ten years, she became an expert at repairing and maintaining. Understanding that her property is an investment, Yvette wanted a house that not only maintained its value but increased in value over time. Below are a few simple actions Yvette took over a ten-year period:

- Maintained landscaping

- Cleaned gutters

- Changed filters to the HVAC system every two months

- Stained and sealed deck wood

- Power-washed siding

- Applied driveway sealer and repaired driveway cracks

Sam hadn't been very proactive about taking care of his property. He saw problems with his house but never dealt with them.

When Sam and Yvette were ready to sell their houses, they hired the same real estate agent, who looked at both homes to determine a listing price. Yvette's home listed for $320,000. Unfortunately, Sam could only list his house for $227,000. Let's look at why there was such a difference in home values.

After ten years of neglecting routine maintenance on his home, Sam's home had problems.

He never liked doing landscaping work, so vines and trees had taken over areas next to the house and property. Over the years, pervasive vines had damaged his downspouts and siding and even pushed their way under the roof shingles. Along with damage from vines, trees planted too close to the house remained problematic for years. On windy days, limbs repeatedly battered the house, causing an estimated $40,000 in damage.

Sam also never cleaned his gutters. Because of this neglect, rainwater had been streaming off the roof and falling beside the house's foundation, causing cracks in the foundation. The cracked foundation caused leaks in the basement and damage to basement floors and walls. Total cost for foundation repairs and new gutters: about $28,000.

The HVAC inspection was another unfortunate experience for Sam. Since he never changed his filters, mold and bacteria had grown in the ductwork, and the system functioned inefficiently because of the blocked ventilation. The whole system needed replacing, and the ventilation systems needed cleaning, a $15,000 job. Sam was feeling the weight of his neglect.

Sam felt confident about his outside deck, which sat on a scenic half-acre lot next to a forest, a small stream at the edge of his property. Unfortunately for Sam, he neglected maintaining the wood on his deck, and much of it had rotted, needing about $3,000 in repairs.

Yvette's house and Sam's house looked very different as well. Since Yvette occasionally power washed her siding, it looked bright and almost new. Sam never power washed, so his house looked dingy and unattractive. Sam would have to pay $2,000 for a cleaning service to make his house look suitable for sale.

Yvette took care of her driveway. Sam didn't, so cracks became miniature craters. A simple protective coating and patch application would have maintained his driveway. Since that didn't occur, Sam would have to pay $5,000 to resurface the driveway before the sale.

Sam wished he had fixed and maintained his home over the ten years that he lived there. Because he didn't, his home's equity wasn't worth as much as Yvette's. Even though it took Yvette effort to maintain her property, she was in a routine of fixing and maintaining, which paid off for her financially when she was ready to sell.

As for Sam, he learned an expensive lesson. His lackadaisical routine of neglect caught up to him in the end, causing him serious financial stress. His options were to pay for all the repairs needed on his house and get it ready to sell or put his home on the market for a much lower price than necessary.

Yvette would sell her house for $320,000 and have $93,000 extra financial gain compared to the sale of Sam's home. Yvette purchased the house for $200,000. She still owes $100,000 on the mortgage balance. After the sale, she will have $220,000 to help buy another home.

Sam's house listed "as is" for $227,000. He decided not to pay for the repairs identified by the realtor. Sam paid $200,000 for the home. Like Yvette, he still owed $100,000 on his mortgage. After the sale, Sam would have $127,000.

Sam's mistakes were costly, but he learned his lesson: when he finds maintenance issues in his next house, he will not ignore the problems. Instead, he plans to establish a routine of fixing and maintaining his home on a regular schedule.

Most youth will not have to respond to home maintenance concerns any time soon. However, there are aspects of their lives where leaving it or fixing it comes into play.

All youth make mistakes with others. The problem interactions can be like cracks in the driveway or vines attacking the siding of a house. When they make a mistake, do they know how to apologize in a reasonable time? Putting off the apology is never a good idea. If you need to make an apology, don't let it stew. Leaving it might cause more stress over time, or it might never happen. Instead, make the apology in a reasonable time. Teach youth to apologize after they make a mistake.

Thank you should be two words that mentors and mentees use often. When someone does small acts of kindness, they deserve a sincere thank-you. Not saying thank you is like the rotting deck wood. Verbally thanking people is straightforward. Also, take advantage of the opportunity to teach your mentee how to write small thank-you notes. Many people send electronic thank-you messages in email or text. There's nothing wrong with that; however, a handwritten thank-you is unique. It takes more effort to handwrite a note, and the receiver will notice and appreciate that extra effort. Teach your mentee to follow through and take action in a reasonable time.

Mentors have an excellent opportunity to demonstrate the routine of checking in. Checking in on your mentee delivers a message that you care. Teach them the same process. What do we mean by checking in? Perhaps a young person finds out that a family member or friend isn't feeling well. Putting off checking on them might result in not checking in on them at all. A check-in routine is personable. Check-ins can be done in person or through other types of communication. The point is to make sure that the person being checked on feels valued and important to you. Please check in regularly with your mentee, and teach them how to manage this people skill.

Finally, youth will benefit from learning the routine of providing enough time to complete a task. Does your mentee have a practice of cramming? If a young person constantly waits until the last minute and then crams to get something done, they might need to learn a new routine. Some people enjoy the stress of waiting until the last minute to complete a project, but not all people can produce quality results by doing this. Teach them to look at this process from a quality perspective. The routine of cramming doesn't provide an opportunity to understand and learn information at a high level.

When a young person decides to put off the hard job of studying or completing a project, they have created a problem. With a more proactive routine, cramming problems can be avoided.

Routines are critical in the process of life. A person who sees and understands routine opportunities has an invaluable problem-solving ability. When they know the value of constantly improving their routines, the youth will think at higher levels.

Touch It One Time

Habits and routines that make life more efficient are terrific life lessons for youth. *Touch it one time* is a rule that might take them through adolescence into adulthood more efficiently.

Most people search for ways to be more productive. We can decrease productivity with poor use of time and procrastination. Touching something just one time may be just what your mentee needs to think about and implement.

Have you ever caught yourself sorting the same mail more than once? I get lazy and sometimes do this. I reach into the mailbox and pull out a handful of mail. Some of it is junk; most of the rest are bills. Taking the stack of mail and setting it on the table, I consider the most effective way to deal with the bill-and-junk-mail intrusion in my life.

The best way to deal with mail is to touch it once. The worst way to deal with the mail is to put it on the table and not have an efficient process of getting it off the table. If you have a desk that piles up with paperwork, the mail concept probably relates just as well. A pile of mail isn't practical storage. There is a better way to deal with mail and other paperwork that piles up.

Use the *touch it one time* rule as your guiding process. Scan an envelope to see if it's junk mail or important correspondence. It would help if you tried only to touch an envelope one time.

Sometimes important letters may require time to read the message thoroughly, and you may not have time to take immediate action. Secure those letters, but don't procrastinate about dealing with them.

You should open junk mail immediately, touching it just one time. To prevent scammers from diving into my trash can for junk mail with my name on it, I shred any junk mail with my name and address. The envelope and other parts of the mail that don't identify information about me get thrown into the recycling can. The junk mail is gone. I don't have to sort it again to determine whether it's junk mail.

What about important mail? It would help if you had a secure place for important correspondence. Suppose I get a bill from the power company. I open the bill, recycle the envelope, and secure the bill in a file. To decrease this process and the paper, I request electronic statements and invoices.

Some people like to pay the bill immediately, a great *touch it one time* scenario. Sometimes I don't have the time to pay the bill immediately. However, the bill will not be in a pile somewhere. Rather, it's secured in its designated spot, and I know exactly where and when to get it.

Young people may not have bundles of junk mail coming in. Instead, they probably have an inbox for email or other online communication. Even with electronic mail, they can learn and use the *touch it one time* routine, immediately deleting junk email and securing or responding to important messages. We all can become more effective by creating folders for important emails.

I like to keep a to-do folder for emails I can't respond to immediately. Using this type of folder requires discipline, however, with the user scheduling a time to respond to the messages in the folder.

Imagine what can happen if you lack the discipline to monitor the to-do folder. Your boss sends you an email that requires action. You put it in the to-do folder but forget that part of the process requires going back and taking action. No one wants to respond to the angry boss following up for a response. To avoid dealing with an angry boss, I schedule reminders in the system to ensure I don't forget important activities.

I once set up a special junk mail folder to decrease junk mail coming into my email platform. I found it essential to check that folder initially because I didn't want important emails accidentally forwarded to the new folder. I'm glad I did this because I found a message from my supervisor in the folder. I had to make a few adjustments to correct the technology mistake, but ultimately it worked well to decrease the number of times I had to touch and look at unimportant information.

Try teaching your mentee the strategy of touching it one time. We know the importance of taking action instead of procrastinating. The path to productivity is to move forward with the job. Youth can learn this essential skill from us.

Chapter 23

Note-Taking

T he design and format of your note-taking depends on you. You will determine what works best. For example, maybe you take electronic notes. Others may use a pen and pencil to take notes. The usability of the end product is the most crucial part of the note-taking process. But what if your boss told you to refrain from taking notes using your preferred method?

My new supervisor, Mr. Howard, briskly walked into the room. "It's good to see you all. I'm glad everyone was able to make it." He paused for a moment in front of the group and scanned the eighty staff members. "Let's start by putting all your electronic devices away now! You're not going to be looking at devices while I'm talking."

The room was alive, with staff quickly grabbing at cell phones and computers. Everyone understood Mr. Howard's message. For most people in the room, it meant they would not send any emails or text messages during the meeting.

Since this group only met for a meeting once a month, taking good notes was essential. Unfortunately, I took notes on an electronic device, a system that was now not an option. This meeting was not going to be easy. You might think I should have interrupted Mr. Howard's presentation and shared my concern. At the time, Mr. Howard spoke as if he were a military general directing his troops before the battle. It was not the time or place to share my note-taking preference with him. I pulled out a sheet of paper and prepared to take notes manually.

Like the situation I encountered with my supervisor, youth may have their specific note-taking style. Taking good notes is an important skill to teach our mentees. Figure out what works for them, and then look for ways to help them improve their process. In some school settings, teachers dictate how students must take notes, but most teachers are very flexible when it comes to the method.

Attributes

Why is note-taking necessary? People need to recall and use information from meetings, workshops, class presentations, and more. A video or audio recording of a presentation might be a fantastic way of recording information, but it's very time-consuming. Notes allow a person to record information efficiently. This information then becomes a resource for the future. In the classroom, youth need to understand that their notes will become a resource they'll use later for studying. They also can use their notes to complete in-class activities.

For those employed, we understand the need to document important information shared during presentations. Your boss expects things to get done. Only some things are neatly put into a memorandum or written in formal regulations and policies. Sometimes you need to document records to move forward with the action item.

Learning Pursuit Pointer #23

Note-taking is a skill that can be used in school and beyond.

I've worked with student programs that strongly recommend specific note-taking skills, such as Cornell notes. Cornell notes might be perfect for some people. For others, there might be a better way. The person must understand why note-taking is necessary and learn some note-taking fundamentals. For example, note-taking should be fun yet give the notetaker confidence that their skills will help them in the future.

It's logical to see how most of a young person's notes will be for personal use only. They take notes of a math formula and use the information in class and outside of class, for example. There are also times a youth might share the notes with others, like when they help to record events.

Youth must also learn to take notes to use as study resources. Regardless of their method, we can share strategies and then encourage mentees to personalize their note-taking to make it work best for them.

Readable

What opportunities about note-taking should you pass along to your mentee? First, the notes should be readable. Readability is a fundamental aspect of all note-taking. Notes will only have value if you can read them.

Accurate

Accuracy is also very important, particularly when notes are used for studying. Creating a system to document information accurately will become easier for a person later as they progress and use note-taking as a tool.

Note-taking is less accurate than video or audio. However, practice and awareness can lead to effective note-taking. It must be a priority for the person taking notes, and they must be able to evaluate their notes for accuracy.

Accessible

I recommend another note-taking requirement for mentors to share. They need to be able to access the information. That sounds simple, but I have worked with youth who needed help finding note resources. They needed to organize their notebooks so they could locate the information quickly.

Organized

This process of notebook organization can take on a personal preference, but it's crucial. When notes are organized, the information is most useful.

Fun

I mentioned earlier that note-taking should be fun for the person taking the notes. After learning how to personalize note-taking and use design and format strategies that work for them, notetakers will consider the process like art, like a painter with a blank canvas. Painters look at a blank canvas differently than someone without art skills. They begin with the end in mind and imagine what they are going to create. Imagine note-taking as fun and creative. When note-taking, we should all have the pleasure of feeling like an artist.

Although young people need to learn to personalize their note-taking, they must still be aware of the improvement process. As they experiment with different designs and systems of note-taking, they should continue to evaluate what works and what doesn't. If you work with your mentee on note-taking fundamentals, provide them with feedback and ask specific questions about success and problems. With the evaluation process, they might improve and become proficient and effective at note-taking.

Different Methods

We all have personal preferences in note-taking. Youth are no exception.

Shirley is a student who likes to consider her note-taking as a blank canvas. She is creative and enjoys learning. She also understands how important it is to use note-taking to help her study for upcoming tests and prepare for class assignments.

Shirley leaned forward at her desk. Scanning the room, she quickly moved her gaze to the teacher. When presenting information, Mr. Carter is an enthusiastic teacher and hurries through topics. The class isn't all presentations. Instead, there are many hands-on activities, but the presentations are critical. Shirley knew she would have to listen closely and take notes during Mr. Carter's opening lecture.

"I believe you all know how important this information is going to be for your upcoming test," Mr. Carter said as he paced back and forth at the front of the classroom. "You need to be ready for our upcoming test. The information will also help you as you work on the lab activity, so let's get started."

Shirley grabbed a stylus for her electronic tablet, as she was very comfortable using this type of device to take notes. *I'm glad Mr. Carter shared that this information will be helpful in the lab and on the test. I'm ready*, Shirley thought.

You're the observer in the room watching a highly effective educator teach and observe two students taking notes during a presentation.

Next to Shirley sits Joanne. Joanne also has a personal preference for note-taking. She writes on lined paper that fits into a three-ring binder labeled by subject. She also has colored markers, colored pencils, regular pencils, and pens on her desk. Both students are ready to take notes.

Mr. Carter started with the objective for the day. He wrote the objective on the classroom blackboard, so both students wrote it in their notes. Shirley used the electronic tablet toolbar to highlight the objective in yellow. The electronic notes allow her to write directly on the tablet. The program enables highlighting, copying, and pasting functions and allows creative note-taking design.

"Our standard for the day deals with the atmosphere. The atmosphere has properties that can be observed, measured, and used to predict changes in weather. We will also identify climate patterns," said Mr. Carter as he moved to the board at the front of the room and pointed to the standard. "It's important for you to understand that the purpose of this lesson is to calculate relative humidity from dew point and temperature measurements." He quickly wrote this information on the board.

Both students wrote Mr. Carter's standards and purpose in their notebooks. Joanne underlined *relative humidity.* She then drew a line with an arrow to the question "What is relative humidity?"

At the same time, Shirley drew a red star next to the temperature measurements. She drew a second star at the bottom of her page and wrote, "How will we measure temperature?"

Walking to the middle of the classroom, Mr. Carter asked, "What typically happens when the relative humidity hits one hundred percent?"

Shirley and Joanne immediately wrote this question into their notes. Shirley circled the question, while Joanne drew a square in front of the question. Joanne then colored the inside of the square with a green pencil.

As observers, we see differences between Shirley's and Joanne's note-taking. There is no standard note-taking requirement, yet both students seemed proficient at note-taking.

After discussing relative humidity, the teacher moved to a graphic display projected at the front of the room. The graph provided students with an opportunity to observe a linear representation of the amount of water air can hold at various temperatures. Mr. Carter discussed the graph and presented many questions. "How many at ten degrees Celsius?" Shirley and Joanne quickly wrote this question and continued using various design elements in their note-taking process. Both were drawing and labeling the graphs.

Color saturated various parts of the note pages. Both students used unique symbols. Both students then took a digital photograph of the teacher's display. Joanne used her cell phone to jot down a note in her notebook: "See the photo of the graph." Shirley used the electronic tablet to take a photograph and immediately pasted the image on the note page.

Just before the students moved into a lab situation, Shirley and Joanne got the chance to compare notes.

"Shirley did a nice job of designating the different steps with an outline format on the right side of the screen. She highlighted the formatting with fun symbols. I think I'll try to use this type of designation the next time I take notes," noted Joanne.

"Joanne has a unique way of using color in her notes to categorize. Different sections stand out nicely. I need to use color more effectively in my note-taking," commented Shirley. "It will be easier for me to find information for studying."

Although Shirley and Joanne used different formatting tools to design their notes, they captured the same information to help them study for the upcoming lab and test. In addition, they formatted their notes in a way that allowed them to be creative. No one told them how to utilize lines, arrows, symbols, graphic organizers, titles, and documentation of facts. Instead, they used the fundamentals of note-taking to help them learn in this class and others.

Design and Format Elements

No matter the method used to take notes, the main goal is to organize the notes to use them at a future date. The design and formatting should be comfortable for the person taking the notes. Below are a few suggestions for designing and formatting notes.

Lines

Lines are perfect for organizing and sectioning off parts of a page. Lines can connect ideas. Drawing a line with an arrow from one point to another is an excellent way to show a connection.

Graphic Organizers

Graphic organizers can add clarity to notes. I recommend that all notetakers use a few favorite graphic organizer structures. New notetakers might like Venn diagrams, T-charts, concept maps, sequence charts, main idea webs, KWL charts (What do you **know**? What do you **want** to know? What have you learned?), cause and effect, and story maps. Notetakers can be creative when learning the best uses for the note-taking tools.

Symbols

Symbols help designate specific information. Like drawing lines, symbols can show a link between items. Symbols can define areas of importance or statements. Be creative with your symbols. A simple bullet point may be effective, but it might be fun to utilize triangles, squares, stars, asterisks, and more. Like the other note-taking strategies, experiment with symbols to improve note-taking organization.

Draw

Drawing skills are not universal, but your mentee may not know the power of drawing while taking notes. Even if not an artist, drawing simple shapes and three-dimensional objects can come in handy. Tell your mentee to relax and have fun in the drawing process. It doesn't have to be perfect or art quality, but it should be readable to them. The notetaker must know what the drawing represents when using drawing skills as a resource.

Color

Colors on the walls can change the dynamic of a room. Color has that same effect in note-taking. Shirley and Joanne used color to draw attention to similar items. Teach your mentee to use color highlighters and pencils along with a simple description (description key) of what the color means. Yellow highlighting might be one category, while blue highlighting could be words you don't know. Green highlighting may be a way to identify an area of note-taking that links to the textbook. Students add color to improve the usefulness of the notes. Without color identifiers, notes are harder to navigate.

Underline

Like color and symbols, underlining helps draw a person's eye into specific parts of the notes. Your mentee may find it helpful to underline essential words in the notes.

Shapes

Circles and other shapes can also be important tools in the note-taking process. Let your mentee identify a specific purpose for circling a section in the text. Like the other descriptive tools, notetakers should use a description key to communicate the purpose of the design.

Pictures

Pictures can be copied and pasted into digital notes. When using paper, a picture could be printed and secured with tape or glue. Also, I like using references in my notes that link to separate images or documents. For example, I will write messages like, "see page 25 photo" or "see ABC1 on page 26." I write in light pencil "ABC1" next to the image on page 26. This type of reference tells me where to go for the image.

Questions

While note-taking, all students find times when a question comes to mind. Questioning should be a fundamental part of note-taking. In the description key, each student should label the color or the symbol for a question. Notetakers can write questions anywhere on the notes or in a specific area of the notes page, but they must take action and get the answer. In addition, they should have some space for an answer. I like to write the question close to the corresponding region of the notes and then identify it with a colored highlighter. *When, where, who, how, would, can, why,* and *what* are good question starters.

Youth can use various resources to answer questions: textbooks, the library, the internet, notes, study groups, and more. However, hopefully, your mentee will consider their teacher as the number one resource to answer questions.

Journaling

Journaling is an effective note-taking method because it allows for creativity and higher-level thinking. I support practicing writing skills because it improves one's writing. Journaling usually is sequential. If the information documented is accurate and allows the writer easy access to essential information, journaling can work well as a note-taking tool.

Sequential Information Documentation

Sequential documentation is a note-taking skill that is very useful when documenting events. When I would observe teachers in the classroom, my note-taking was sequential and scripted. I would write down things as they occurred. When the teacher or a child said something, I would document that information in quotations. This type of note-taking allowed me to relive the time in the room. Using those notes, I was able to create an evaluative feedback document. It was not as good as a video, but the process allowed me to help the teacher improve.

Young people might benefit from this type of sequential note-taking. Most schools require students to use agenda books or other scheduling tools. Many may also have access to technology tools that facilitates note-taking. When they have good or bad interactions with others, they can document the date, time, and incident as a record.

I would share this strategy with youth during bullying situations. Bullied students would use sequential note-taking to document the problem. When adults need to intervene and help, the sequential information tells a story over time. The following information would help me understand what was happening:

- When did the incident occur (date and time)?

- Where did the incident occur?

- Who was there?

- What happened (physical actions and comments made by all the people involved)?

For many bullying situations, a young person might be able to handle the problem by themselves. However, in more severe cases, a youth might want help to solve the problem. I like to see young people solve problems, but there are times when an adult might need to assist. Notes are beneficial in problem-solving efforts because they show events and patterns of behavior over time.

Note-taking is a strategy that will help a young person beyond the school setting. Personalizing and figuring out what works best takes time and openness to creativity. After deciding on the best design and format to use, the notetaker should consider having fun with the notes. The work that they put into their notes is like a painting, though it's a vital resource. Notetakers should experiment with questions and make sure that they follow up to get the questions answered. Finally, the notetaker must find what works best. They may need help from us to evaluate the process and look for opportunities to improve.

Chapter 24

More Life Skills to Teach

I t's never too early to teach life skills to young people. We can utilize fun activities and experiences to emphasize the importance of thinking and planning before an event or activity.

Our family was excited about the upcoming vacation. We were going to the city and had a plan for different activities and fun-filled days.

My two young daughters were beyond excited about going on vacation! They were accommodating when I shared with them the importance of thinking and planning to ensure the vacation's outcome was a success, and they quickly agreed to my planning meeting. Success!

I like to double up my activities. Vacations are fun, but they can also be exceptional learning experiences.

We started with a list, writing out our goals for the vacation. My daughters quickly pointed out the importance of learning, having fun, respecting each other, and more. It didn't take long for a list to grow.

In addition to our goal list, I shared with them that I would use a list of things to take on vacation to ensure that we had everything we would need to have fun and be comfortable.

Our thinking activity was going well. Next, because of my law enforcement and military background, I shared with them the importance of identifying dangerous situations and communicating the danger with family members.

We brainstormed ideas of what danger might look like. After identifying dangerous situations, we developed signals. One signal was to communicate verbally. We also created a lower-profile hand signal that would not draw the attention of other people. We were on a roll. My daughters knew the signal and understood the communication methods. What could go wrong?

While walking in the city, I was in front of my family. I noticed a physically fit man coming toward us, talking to himself and throwing punches in the air. Some punches were directed at the people walking toward him. He didn't hit anyone, but his punches were close to connecting.

Not wanting to draw his attention, I signaled danger. I looked at my daughters, and they seemed to have observed my signal. However, they made no effort to lower their voices or look for the problem. Instead, they became loud, and I thought they were about to run out in front of me. I acted and got in between my family and this stranger.

After passing the man without incident, my daughters confirmed they saw my signal.

In hindsight, I realize I should have thought through the communication method more. My daughters were too young to navigate the dangerous situation. In their minds, yes, there was a problem; but they knew Dad would handle it.

From that point on, I decided to add a step to my thinking strategies to include "practice"! I should have practiced with my daughters.

On a positive note, we had an excellent vacation and met all our goals on the list. We also learned how important it is to take the time to think and constantly be on the lookout for life skills.

Learning Pursuit Pointer #24
It's never too early to teach life skills to young people.

Lists

Lists are an essential tool for anyone who wants to organize a group of thoughts, words, or numbers. As an organizing tool, your mentee can become more effective by using lists.

As a schoolteacher, an essential tool I used was the attendance list. Each day, students came into the classroom, and I took attendance. A list of names allowed me to record who was there, who was absent, and each student's behavior over time.

Lists help us prepare. Pre-event lists are an example of a helpful preparation tool. As you consider what you need at an event, put those items on a list. By having a list, preparation becomes much easier.

When might a list be helpful to someone young? As we mentor, we need to identify possible organizing problems our mentees might have. Could a list help?

As a coach, there were times when my athletes would come to practice unprepared, often forgetting equipment we needed for practice. For example, athletes sometimes forgot a mouthpiece, headgear, sneakers, and even the uniform. A list might have helped. If your mentee is prone to forgetfulness, they should create a list.

If a young person travels several times throughout the week or months, they might find it beneficial to have a list as they prepare. Reviewing the list will help ensure they don't leave essential items behind.

If I visit relatives in another state, I have a list of items I need to bring along, and I quickly look at the list to make sure that I have everything before exiting my house.

Adults, more often than youth, will find themselves presenting to groups. If you're in a leadership role, you know the equipment and materials you will need for a presentation. If you use a presentation equipment list, share it with your mentee. This might give them ideas about how a list can make them more effective. My list includes projectors, extension cords, flip chart paper, and many other items used for a workshop.

As a workshop presenter, I shared an equipment storage space with other presenters. I thought my equipment box and bags were ready to go, but, unfortunately, that wasn't always true. Equipment was sometimes missing because other presenters would use the equipment and not return it to the storage area. I solved the problem with a list. By utilizing a list, I was always confident that my equipment was ready when I needed it.

Do you utilize a to-do list? The to-do list is different from the goal-setting record. My weekly goal-setting activities link to my personal mission statements and my roles. My to-do list might connect to my mission, but it includes other to-do actions as well. Writing things down on a list helps me get things done. Your mentee may experience this exact outcome.

The grocery list is my last example to help you teach about the benefits of a list. I could not function without a grocery list. Whenever I start running low on a grocery item, I write down what needs to be purchased. The list is a perfect reminder for the next trip to the store.

Lists are valuable tools. Give your mentee an opportunity how to brainstorm areas where lists might be helpful.

Think Before You Act — Receivers of the Message

Young people may need help understanding how their actions affect others. If we get youth thinking in this way, we help them in decision-making and problem-solving.

How can a simple decision affect others? What will happen if they don't complete a group school project and decide instead to go to the mall with friends. Even though they know the project is due the following day, they don't always think ahead.

It's fun to go to the local mall with friends. It's less fun completing a project. The group project is due tomorrow, and our young mentee has responsibility for completing specific parts of the project. Going to the local mall is a mistake because it affects not just the youth but also others in the group. Other team members in the group may receive a lower grade because one member chose to pursue fun instead of completing the project. The young person was not thinking ahead.

Initially, the undisciplined youth in this scenario may believe they only created a problem for teammates. Each of the group members, however, has a parent. Those parents now see the lower grade produced by the group. Some of the parents are not pleased, and several contact the teacher with formal complaints, wanting to meet with the teacher to discuss the grade.

The mall decision has caused more people to get involved. It seemed like a simple decision to go to the mall with friends. Was it worth the visit? Suddenly, that decision led to a more significant problem. Parents scheduled a meeting with the teacher. The teacher gave a lower grade to the group and now must explain the grade. Parents weren't satisfied with the meeting and didn't like the teacher's explanation, so they took their concerns to the assistant principal. The assistant principal met with the parents and teacher. Following the meetings, the assistant principal decided to uphold the low grade given for the project. Not satisfied still, the parents moved it to the next level of the appeal process: the head principal.

Consider how one decision affected so many people.

We need to make it clear that thinking first goes with decision-making. Mentees must consider who will be affected by the decision. The young person should not have gone to the local shopping mall. Instead, they should have completed the project. They now know that their overall grade may suffer because of their poor decision. They also are aware the decision will negatively affect team members. A good decision would have made parents and teammates happy.

Think Before You Act

As you explore other ways to help your mentee think before they act, consider the outcome of a poorly written and sent text message. Before sending a text message, review the questions below to help your mentee avoid unintended repercussions:

- Who is the intended recipient?

- Is the message communicating what you want to convey?

- Could the message be misunderstood?

- Is the purpose of the message clear?

- If the message receiver forwards the message to others, what will happen? Will unintended readers misinterpret the message?

- If the message communicates a decision, will the decision trigger problems?

- Have you sent similar messages? What did you learn from previous communications?

After hitting send, it's usually too late to change anything, so it's always wise to think first before hitting send. That fundamental principle can also help in decision-making. Teach the skill to young people to help them become better problem solvers. It's empowering to control the results of decisions and messages by thinking first. Decision-makers want to hit the intended target.

We are not in control of many things in life. But for each of us, thinking before acting is within our control. It is a fundamental component of self-control. I like to be in control of my destiny. I also enjoy helping young people learn that they also have control. Actions lead to consequences.

Effective Decision-Makers Think First

From an observer perspective, the great Olympians appear to make physical movement and performance look effortless. Consider the world-class Olympian in the sport of archery. They know how to hit the target and make shooting an arrow into the center of a target look easy. The casual observer only sees the arrow flying into the center of the target, not the many steps that happen before the arrow is even released. Those critical steps are necessary for the arrow to stay on target.

Like the best archers, we need to think before making decisions so that the outcome doesn't go off target. People who make good decisions have self-control. The opposite is true for those who don't make good decisions. Poor decision-makers seem to need more self-control. Effective decision-makers think before they act.

Why do Olympic archers want to perfect the tiny movements before the shot? All Olympians love to win, and they know that competition is a part of the process. They understand that it's their job to shoot arrows into the middle of the target. Scores matter in archery.

Decision-makers need to know the outcome or the target they want. Why does the decision have to be made? Whether it's a small or big decision, we need awareness of the actions and outcome. We need to take action to achieve something.

Even though there are time constraints in archery competitions, archers will focus on small details like foot positioning or stance. Without a proper posture, the shot will be in jeopardy. I have never observed an archer run to the shooting area and launch an arrow without awareness of body position. Even shooters who run and jump while shooting control body position and timing.

Decision-makers also need to be careful with the speed and timing of decision-making. With a more critical decision at stake, planning and thought about the outcome should be handled precisely. Decision-makers can all describe a time when a decision went bad, and often times it was because the decision-maker may have acted too quickly.

The young person who thinks before taking action has an advantage over others. They are aware of self-control and power in decision-making, and they spend time thinking first and focusing on the outcome. Decisions that are not in an emergency environment allow for thinking. However, just like the Olympian, there needs to be action. Olympians need to shoot the arrow. If they wait too long, they will be penalized and lose points. Likewise, there are times when the decision-maker can't wait and action must quickly take place.

In leadership situations, leaders have to make quick decisions. The principle of thinking before you act still applies. People who deal with emergencies prepare and practice before the crisis. That preparation helps them make good decisions during the crisis because they have already considered the problem and solution.

Thinking before you act also involves considering other similar situations and awareness that other people may have feedback for us because of their experiences. You can benefit by reaching out to others to learn what has happened in the past. Experienced mentors are perfectly suited to share life lessons. However, a decision-maker doesn't have to rely totally on a mentor for feedback. We should teach mentees the importance of using the perspectives of others for tough decisions.

Like the Olympic athlete, mentors should look for opportunities for mentees to practice making decisions. The more decisions they make or discuss, the more prepared they will be as decision-makers. For example, you might intentionally discuss current news events, asking questions such as the following:

- Do you think the person was practicing the *think before you act* strategy? Why or why not?

- If you were that person, what would you do next?

- If you were facing that challenge, who would you check with before deciding?

- What could that person have done differently?

- Would you have made the same decision?

- How do you think this situation is going to end?

Decision-makers know that there may be unintentional consequences for a decision. Thinking before you make a decision helps decrease the number of unintended consequences.

The expert archer knows about unintended consequences. Consider, for example, safety in the archery range. An archery range can allow multiple archers to practice shooting simultaneously. Each range has established safety rules because they want to avoid unintended consequences. Archers know from experience that archery is an exceptionally safe sport, but injuries can still occur if everyone isn't following the rules.

Let's look at a few range rules for an archer and consider how archers and decision-makers should avoid unintended consequences. Archers want to avoid pointing an arrow anywhere but downrange to prevent injury. Range managers enforce this simple rule with vigor. Why? Most bows have a string nocking point that guides archers on where to put their arrow nock. On the other side of the arrow nock is the arrowhead. If an archer nocks an arrow, the archer must point the arrowhead downrange, or other people will be at risk. I will leave a shooting range if the other shooters don't follow this rule.

Decision-makers who make poor decisions are like the careless archer who points the arrow down the shooter line rather than downrange. Is a drunk driver like a careless archer? The person who decides to drink and drive puts themself and others in danger.

I've sought creative ways to teach youth the dangers of drugs and alcohol. My doctoral degree research and final project focused on a youth drug and alcohol prevention program. There were many educational components in my prevention curricula and strategies. Getting young people to think first was one of those components.

When young people start to use mind-altering substances, their ability to think decreases, and they become less effective decision-makers. We need to get young people to think before they engage in alcohol and drug use, especially as we influence them not to drive while under the influence (DUI). There are horrendous possible outcomes of driving under the influence.

As a part of my research, in a small-group setting, four high school students and I discussed ways to get young people to think first before driving under the influence. Lack of awareness was not the problem. All students felt strongly that they and their peers knew that driving while intoxicated was terrible. However, they knew of friends who drove while under the influence. Young people who ignore dangerous outcomes are not using the think-first strategy.

One youth commented, "Parents can be scarier than death sometimes." This comment was shared while the youth considered whether to call home for a ride or drive while intoxicated. This type of thinking is like being bumped while shooting an arrow.

Peers can also influence decision-making related to DUI. Peer pressure is a tremendous influence when completely sober. While under the influence, however, peer pressure influence expands and can lead to poor decision-making and disastrous outcomes.

The four young people in my research group shared strategies they thought might change behaviors:

- Year-round continuous messaging

- Student-led organizations to combat DUI

- Messaging from their peers

- Real-world examples of negative outcomes

The student recommendations were helpful as we focused on drug and alcohol prevention at our high school. Our discussions also reinforced the importance of decision-making. Effective decision-makers think first.

Thinking first and being on the lookout for unintentional consequences before making a decision will help a young person navigate through the challenges of adolescence. Just like the archer who has rules and understands why the rules are essential, youth need to respect the power of decisions. They will learn that unintended consequences can come in a variety of ways, even if you're aiming for the target center:

- Missed target because of technique—poor planning

- Something moves in front of the target—lack of awareness

- Someone bumps you while shooting—influence of others

- Ricocheting arrow—results out of your control

Mentors teaching the power of decision-making and thinking first will need to be on the lookout for teaching opportunities. We should look for real-world situations where we can clarify our message.

Think Before You Act — Evaluating the Outcome

Thinking before you act provides an opportunity to consider the results. Using the strategy of *thinking before you act* doesn't mean that every decision will be effective. Instead, you'll sometimes miss the target.

Think again of the archer. The mechanics in archery are very fine-tuned, and small changes in the process of shooting an arrow can change the results. Archers look at their technique in detail. They also have coaches and archers on the same team evaluate their shooting technique.

We should do the same as decision-makers and problem solvers. After teaching your mentee to think first, they should learn to evaluate the results of the decisions. Why did they make the decision? What actions caused the outcome? Was the outcome expected before the decision-making? What went well, and what didn't go well? These are just a few questions to ask in the evaluation process.

It's also important to consider how the decision compares to other experiences. Were there similarities that will provide information in the future? Brainstorming with others about the situation will also lead to better decision-making in the future. Mentor-and-mentee discussions might expand to include others.

I also see value in identifying possible chain reactions that might result from the decision. Did your mentee's actions trigger something or many things? They may not have seen the chain reaction of events coming, but they probably learned from them.

Teaching mentees to think before they act is to share a foundational life skill for self-control that yields substantial benefits. Following a think-first decision, work with your mentee to evaluate the results for improvement. Mentors should be proud to see their mentees think first when facing a challenge.

Chapter 25

Trust

The mentor-mentee relationship is a priority for a mentor. The relationship between the mentee's parent and the mentor is also important. These relationships could be at risk without a structure of trust. Developing trust takes time.

Feeding birds also takes time. When I first put up a bird feeder in my backyard, the birds were unpredictable. Only a few showed up at first. Some showed up to look around but then flew away soon after.

This metaphor of bird visits to my backyard is similar to how we build trust in relationships. New bird feeder platforms are initially foreign to wild birds. The birds are cautious, unsure if it will be safe to perch on the feeder. Just like the birds looking at the bird feeder from a safe perch in a tree, trust in a relationship, in most cases, doesn't happen overnight but is worth waiting for.

Supply Character and Competence Over Time

Trust requires a belief in another person's competence and character. Trust will be low when a person has great character but lacks competence. The same is true when someone is competent but lacks character.

Your character and integrity will be under a microscope during the mentoring process. This is a good thing. If you're a person of character, you will consistently demonstrate your honesty. It does take time to build relationships and for the word to get out in the community that you're a role model.

It was mid-September when Principal Clarke met with all the newly hired teachers. Making his way down the hallway, he walked with a spring in his step. He was looking forward to his meeting with Mr. Ryan. Mr. Ryan was new to the community and school but had a distinguished career in another school nearby. He was known as one of the most respected teachers in that community—kids loved him, and he achieved academic success.

Over the summer, Principal Clarke had an opportunity to interview for a math position. He and the interview committee members were excited when Mr. Ryan applied. After a long and tedious interview process, the interview committee overwhelmingly wanted the position offered to Mr. Ryan. He accepted the offer.

Principal Clarke had visited Mr. Ryan's room many times since the start of the year. From what he observed, the decision to hire Mr. Ryan was a success. Students were engaged and learning math. Now Principal Clarke was going to a pre-evaluation conference with Mr. Ryan. Upon entering the room, he observed educational posters and student work covering the classroom. The room was alive with signs of instruction and included a math resource study library. Comfortable chairs were set in the area and seemed to be a magnet for pulling students to that area of the room. The teaching environment sent a message: this is a great learning place. Principal Clarke imagined sitting in one of the cozy chairs and reading about the men and women who used math to solve scientific and engineering problems.

Mr. Ryan also had written messages to the students on the work displayed throughout the classroom. One assignment had the message, "Jen, I like how you show your work! You're excelling because of your effort and focus on the processes that solve math problems! Super job!"

"Hello, Mr. Ryan!" Mr. Clarke said as he sat down in the chair next to Mr. Ryan's desk.

"Hi, Principal Clarke. I appreciate your visit," Mr. Ryan said in a firm business greeting.

Principal Clarke sensed something was not right. Usually, Mr. Ryan was much more friendly. Mr. Ryan appeared slightly stressed, unhappy, and tired. He wasn't smiling, his arms were crossed, and he didn't make direct eye contact with the principal. Instead, he looked down at the paperwork on his desk. "Thanks again for visiting today, Principal Clarke. I know that you have a busy schedule."

Principal Clarke leaned forward and smiled. "First, it's great to have you on this school team Mr. Ryan! Tell me how things are going. Has the transition to our school been smooth for you and your family?"

Mr. Ryan leaned back in his chair. Still not smiling, he shook his head left and right several times. He now made eye contact with the principal and started talking slowly. "I'm okay. I'm glad you asked. I'm in shock to tell you the truth. I've been teaching for over twenty years. I can't believe how the students and parents in this community seem not to be accepting of me as a teacher."

Principal Clarke's expression changed from a look of positivity to one of concern. He was surprised, to say the least, as that was the last thing he expected to hear. "Tell me more about what's happening. What do you mean that they are not accepting?"

"At C. J. Middle School, I was extremely respected as a teacher. I guess I'm just not used to people not knowing who I am. This community is unaware of my background and expectations for student learning. They are treating me as if I am a brand-new teacher."

Principal Clarke spoke with interest and enthusiasm. "Wow. Okay. This situation must be causing you stress." He leaned forward and smiled. "We're in this together. It may take some time, but you're a skilled and respected teacher, and I know that our community will see how hard you work to help students learn. I will support you in any way to make sure that we get through this transition."

The following months were a challenge. Principal Clarke made it a point to check in with Mr. Ryan routinely. He was a highly effective teacher and a natural at building trusting relationships. Students and parents began to see his skill as a teacher. Although it took some time, he operated with integrity and did not give up. He vented and shared ideas occasionally with the principal, and, ultimately, he earned others' trust and respect as a teacher.

It takes time to build relationships. Mentors may have a similar experience as the example I just shared. It will take time for your mentee, their parents, and the community to get to know who you are. Eventually, the people you influence will talk about your efforts. Those efforts will pay off for the mentee and, in many cases, spread throughout the community. If you have integrity and get results, people will notice.

Let's look back to the bird feeder example to see how it relates to our discussion of trust. After the feeder was in the yard for months, wild birds were no longer scarce and unpredictable. Instead, my visitors were routine and varied: American goldfinch, red-bellied woodpecker, house finch, Carolina chickadee, cardinal, dove, Eastern bluebird, and many more types of birds. The food source was safe, dependable, and consistent. Because of this, they developed a habit of visiting. Their behavior resembled someone with high trust. The birds were comfortable.

Trusting relationships can also become comfortable. Over time, when a person is competent and honest, they become a trusted person. They will not let you down. Integrity alone will not be enough. A person needs to get things done well.

Low Trust Requires Action

What happens when competence or character becomes questionable in a relationship? You may have been in a situation where someone you trusted didn't demonstrate character. You may have also experienced people with high integrity who didn't have the skill to get results. Did your trust in those people go down? Their weakness influenced trust. We all make mistakes. When we do, trust may show some wear and tear but won't sustain permanent damage.

It's essential to clean bird feeders. While cleaning, birds visit and find the feeder gone. Does that mean they will never return? That's not likely. They will come back to the bird feeder if I return the clean feeder with fresh birdseed in a reasonable time.

In the same way, a person who demonstrates minor problems with character and competence can fix the trust relationship. Considering the trust relationship with others, we must remember that people are different. One person may have a substantial tolerance for mistakes. Another person may have a low tolerance level, resulting in a slow regaining of a trusting relationship.

Can the trust between people be broken severely? Certainly. You've probably experienced or know somebody who has experienced a situation where trust was severed because of a lack of honesty or other factors. People make decisions based on facts or perceived facts.

The total breakdown in trust is similar to what I observed with the wild birds that visited my feeder. There was once an alert in the newspapers that a bird illness was a problem in my state. People who fed birds with bird feeders were encouraged to remove their feeders. I took my feeder down and watched the birds perch close to where the feeder used to be. They seemed puzzled that the feeder was gone. It didn't take long for the birds to stop visiting my yard.

When trust is damaged severely, the relationship will be in trouble. If a person isn't competent or honest, they will be like the bird feeder taken away from the wild birds. There was no longer food, so why should they drop in to check?

Eventually, experts lifted bird feeder restrictions in our state. I put the feeder back in my yard, cleaned it out, and put fresh seed out for the birds. I was anxious to see the return of the many types of birds that previously visited, but it didn't happen. After a week, only a few birds showed up at the feeder. The birds were unpredictable in my yard and had moved on to other places. It took time for the birds to return.

Unfortunately, when trust is damaged severely, the relationship may never have the same trust, or there may be no trust. We should take action to avoid damaging our mentoring relationships, always demonstrating high character and competence with mentees and their parents.

The Power of Promise

Our goal as mentors should be to influence young people so that their value system produces excellence. The power of a promise is a part of the life skill mix. Making and keeping that promise is like adding birdseed to a bird feeder. The person making and keeping a promise increases trust in the relationship. Promises have power because the agreement of a promise can create trust between individuals. If you make a promise to yourself and you follow through, you're demonstrating self-discipline.

One way we can teach promise care is with a metaphor about artifacts. Archaeologists look for artifacts that can provide a history. An artifact could be a pot for cooking, a sculpture, or even an arrowhead.

I remember walking through the forest with my grandfather when I was very young, and we were looking for artifacts from an ancient civilization. It was amazing to find arrowheads that were a tool from another time. Although we were not archaeologists, it was exciting when my grandfather found the artifacts. I never was observant or patient enough to unearth any myself, but he did.

Archaeologists research exactly where to look for artifacts. They also practice the art of excavation. Excavation skills include keeping artifacts unharmed.

As an amateur, my grandfather never documented his findings. Archaeologists, however, are extremely focused on recordkeeping. They know the importance of documenting to tell future archaeologists and scientists about the specific archaeologic exploration. How was the artifact discovered? Where was the artifact discovered? Archaeologists record these facts.

Not all archaeologists are out in the field; but those who are in the field are excited about what they're doing and dream of discovering artifacts that will tell them something historical. Although finding artifacts is rare, field archaeologists are enthusiastic about their possibilities. We should be equally enthusiastic and caring about our promises, handling them with care as though they are newly discovered artifacts.

Tools of the trade for archaeology include a trowel, dustpan, skewer, brushes, buckets, and screens. Archaeologists use their tools to solve big problems. This is a very time-intensive process, for they can work for extended amounts on something that either could be an artifact or not.

Image seeing a hard substance in the earth. You need to find out what it is. Using brushes and wooden skewers, you slowly remove the soil. After hours of work, you don't know if the hard substance is an artifact or a rock. However, you focus intently on not destroying what might be an artifact. If you move too fast or with too much intensity, you might damage the artifact. To damage an artifact in the field is to have destroyed a piece of history. You could glue things back together, but it wouldn't be the same. Imagine how upset the lead archaeologist would be with you. Broken artifacts cause stress.

Broken promises can also cause stress. Each promise is a gift to us or someone else. We need to have self-control and deliver on our promise. If we don't, we are damaging something. The person to whom we made a promise will probably lose trust in us. Likewise, if we make promises to ourselves and don't follow through, we lose self-confidence.

Like the damaged artifact, not following through damages our ability to demonstrate self-control.

In the field of archaeology, the people in the field are usually young. Digging in the soil is a physical job that can be taxing, so you don't usually see elderly archaeologists. Field archaeologists are always learning. Hopefully, if they damage an artifact, their supervisor will help them learn how not to damage another one.

But what if the field archaeologist continues to break artifacts? The supervisor will lose trust. Artifacts are hard to come by, and damaging an artifact is a big problem.

An equally big problem is for us to refrain from following through on our promises to others. One time might dent the trust between you and another, but several broken promises will have a more significant effect. Like the field archaeologists digging in the dirt, much depends on our ability to deliver a promise. We need to be careful with our promises and teach our mentees how to demonstrate self-control in making and keeping their promises as well.

Field archaeologists are not always responsible for finding a place to unearth artifacts and dig. Specialists often identify the best areas to conduct archaeological digging. Without the specialists, finding artifacts would be infrequent. So how do the specialists determine the best places to dig? First, they review the documentation from other archaeologists. Without documentation, they might rely on other sources like remote sensing, ground surveys, aerial surveys, and satellite surveys.

People who never make promises might need to consider the archaeologist specialist who finds good spots to dig. Where are the trusting relationships in your life? Can you build trust in those relationships? At times, you may need to make a promise. If you never make a promise, you might miss out on an action that reveals character.

Learning Pursuit Pointer #25

When you make a promise, you need to follow through.
This demonstrates self-control.

We should provide our mentees with the right message. It is important to make promises and follow through on those promises. It is also not characteristic of people to never make a promise. Make a promise like a person uncovering soil from a rare artifact. In the right environment, making promises is good and healthy.

As mentors, we know the importance of teaching the art of self-discipline. Teaching how to promise is one example of self-discipline that mentees will benefit from for the rest of their lives. Also, mentors need the discipline to include others in the mentoring process. The parent-and-mentor relationship is an example of a partnership, a relationship built on trust. Mentors should promise to include the parent and follow through on that promise.

Chapter 26

Conclusion

Whether in a formal mentoring program or mentoring someone outside of a program, you are needed. Looking for ways to help others is always a worthwhile endeavor. Our youth need direction, and you are special because you care about the growth of others.

My life has changed drastically because many people have guided me. I fondly remember many mentors and teachers who took the time to encourage me at a young age. Several of the teachers also coached. Athletic teams taught me about teamwork and leadership. I watched how the coaches worked with us and learned the great benefits of a team situation.

Teachers like Mr. Earl Bodes, Mr. William Hough, and Mr. Thomas Reeve were my industrial arts teachers in high school. I enjoyed attending school because of them and their classes. They may not have known they were influencing and mentoring me then. Because of their teaching, I believed that there was no technology that I could not learn. I hope they would be proud to know that I went on to be a technology education teacher.

Mr. James Martz was my principal in high school. He was always available to students and became a mentor to me as he took the time to follow my athletic and academic activities. I eventually earned a few dollars from him by mowing his grass. Mr. Martz shared with me many leadership ideas and inspired me to look for leadership opportunities. He also constantly reminded me that I could do whatever I wanted and that my dreams could come true if I visualized and set my mind to it. I greatly appreciate the wisdom of Mr. Martz and the time he gave to me.

After high school, unfortunately, I drifted away from adult mentors. Instead, I was following other young people. We influenced each other, and I headed down the wrong path of life. *Mentor them, or they will* is something I experienced. Young people should look to successful adults to find the way to a successful life. I should have searched for and found adult mentors immediately after high school. Thankfully, I was able to redirect and get my life back together by reaching back into my past and remembering principles my mentors taught. They taught me not to give up when things get tough.

Mr. Bodes was detail oriented. He continually shared with me the importance of being exact and not sloppy.

Mr. Hough taught lessons about endurance. When challenges come—and they *will* come—we must always press forward and never give up.

Mr. Reeve provided me with a template for setting challenging goals and succeeding. There was always a plan, but adjustments were essential to success.

I was able to draw on what was taught early in my life to move forward and out of a toxic path. I've had many mentors in my life, and I will always appreciate the time and effort they put into helping me along the way. I often think of their lessons and try to share them with others.

Be Encouraged: Your Influence May Carry Forward

As you work to develop life skills with a young person, you may not see the results of your efforts immediately, but mentees may remember your time and what you shared. Don't get discouraged or give up. Continue to work with them and enjoy the process. You never know what nuggets of information will connect and help them in the future.

Learning Pursuit Pointer #26

We are responsible for our choices.

Other mentees may appear to grasp everything you share yet still take wrong turns in life. They may experience challenges with academics or even the criminal justice system. Don't take it personally. Each of us makes and is responsible for our own choices in life.

Look for Mentoring Opportunities

I had many challenges as a youth. It would be easy for me to reflect on my youth and point out people who may have helped send me on the wrong path. That type of thinking is wrong. I take responsibility for my problems and bad decisions.

While interviewing an incarcerated man in prison, I found that he had the same perspective. He took responsibility for his actions and was trying to change his life and the lives of others. He volunteered to present to young people because he didn't want others to make the same mistakes he made.

This inmate commented to me that he had a dream for his children: "Children mentoring children doesn't work. We need positive adult role models to mentor."

He was looking back on his life. He didn't have substantial adult role models. Instead, he drifted to other youth in the community who also didn't have guidance. Those bad influences shaped his value system, and legal problems followed.

Teachers, coaches, mentors, and parents should all understand that they are responsible for guiding our youth. Without an understanding of principles and moral values, youth could end up with so many problems that could have been avoided with good guidance.

I challenge you to look for mentoring opportunities in your community. Mentoring can make a tremendous difference in a young person's life. And remember, mentor them, or *they* will.

Acknowledgments

The author would like to thank the dedicated team whose contributions helped make this book a reality:

Brainstorming Team

My super smart and beautiful daughters, Elyse and Kyra

Copy and Line Editor

Rebecca Franks

Cover Designer

Jamie Tipton, Open Heart Designs

Developmental Editor

Ella Ritchie, Stellar Communications Houston

Proofreader

Elizabeth Hudgins

About the Author

Chad Carmack is a former school principal who recognized the opportunity to change lives by mentoring, identifying untapped potential, and taking action to help individuals grow.

A pivotal moment in Chad's teaching career changed his professional path. Before becoming a principal, he was a technology education teacher passionate about mentoring and teaching the most challenging students. Many of his students struggled in other courses but excelled in his class, as they loved hands-on activities and technology topics. Chad found a way to spark their interests. When he displayed a group photo of student leaders and their work, a colleague approached him and said, "They are a bunch of criminals." Chad knew he would have to step into a leadership position to change this type of thinking. He became a principal to cultivate highly effective teachers and facilitate school-wide student academic achievement initiatives while championing the power of mentorships.

Chad served thirty years in public education as a principal, assistant principal, human resources specialist, and technology education teacher. After serving four years in the United States Air Force, he studied at Millersville University in Pennsylvania where he received his bachelor of science in education. While working as an educator, he completed his master of business administration at Wilmington University in Wilmington, Delaware, and his doctor of education in educational leadership at the University of Delaware in Newark, Delaware.

Chad is the founder of Learning Pursuit, LLC.

Join the Community

I invite you to join our growing and dynamic Learning Pursuit team. Subscribe to our newsletter at https://www.learningpursuit.org/subscribe to receive regular updates. As a member, you'll receive exclusive updates on my latest essays, videos, and valuable resources crafted to inspire character development, leadership growth, and impactful youth mentoring. Our Learning Pursuit community is more than just feedback and resources from me. Each member of our community can contribute and help us improve the quality of our information on becoming highly effective mentors and leaders. Please join our community and help shape our future!

Feedback About the Book

As I launch my debut book, *Mentor Them or They Will*, I am committed to constant improvement and always seeking learning opportunities. Your feedback is extremely valuable to me and will greatly assist me in shaping my future writings. Whether it's positive or constructive, please do share your thoughts, and know that you're contributing to my growth and improvement as a writer. Thank you for being a part of this collaborative process.

Contact Information

Website: https://www.learningpursuit.org

Email address: info@learningpursuit.org

Newsletter subscription: https://www.learningpursuit.org/subscribe

Connect with the Author and Subscribe!

Join the Learning Pursuit community at https://www.learningpursuit.org!

We're thrilled to welcome you to the Learning Pursuit team. Subscribe to our newsletter for exclusive content, the latest insights, free resources, and news of upcoming events.

Connect with us through our website's contact page to schedule a coaching session or book an event. Your journey toward learning and growth begins here!

Bibliography

Agriculture, United State Department of. 2022. https://www.fns.usd a.gov/building-back-better-school-meals#FAQ . March 28. Accessed March 28, 2022.

Arain M, Haque M, Johal L, Mathur P, Nel W, Rais A, Sandhu R, Sharma S. 2013, Published and Licensed by Dove Medical Press Limited. "Maturation of the Adolescent Brain." Saint James School of Medicine, Kralendijk, Bonaire, The Netherland 1.

Armstrong, Maj. General Spence M. 1983. "From the commander." Basic military training handbook. United States Air Force.

Armstrong, Thomas. 2016. The Amazing Adolescent Brain. Alexandria, VA: ASCD.

Armstrong, Thomas. 2016. The Power of the Adolescent Brain, Strategies for Teaching Middle and High School Students. Alexandria, VA: Association of Supervision and Curriculum Development.

Blaettler, Karen G. 2018. The Manufacturing Process of Rubber. December 15. Accessed July 27, 2022.

CH, Johnston-Brooks. 1998 Sep-Oct. "Chronic stress and illness in children: the role of allostatic load. doi: 10.1097/00006842-1998090 00-00015. PMID: 9773764." Psychosom Med. 60(5):597-603.

Dewberry, Tech. Sgt. Joshua. 2021. Air Force unveils new mission statement. April 8. Accessed June 14, 2023.

Frankl, Viktor E. 1985. Man's Search For Meaning. New York: Washington Square Press.

Guralnik, David B. 1976. Webster's New World Dictionary of the American Language. New York: Simon and Schuster.

Indianapolis Freeman. 1899. "Dr. Josep W. Ward." July 22: 1 and 4.

Jensen, Eric. 2008. Brain-Based Learning The New Paradigm of Teaching. California: Corwin Press.

n.d. Jesse Owens Memorial Park Links and Facts. Accessed June 15, 2023.

Koch, Richard. 1998. The 80/20 Principle The Secret To Success By Achieving More With Less. New York: Doubleday.

1910. "Lectured to Frenchmen." The Chanute Daily Tribune. Chanute: Tribune Publishing Company, April 23.

Life, Richard Johnson/Outdoor. 2012. Outdoor Life The Ultimate Survival Manual. San Francisco: Weldon Owen.

Norton, Holly. 2002. "School skate club a first." The News Journal. Wilmington: A Gannett Newspaper, November 16.

Pierce J. Howard, Ph. D. 2014. The Owner's Manual for the Brain The Ultimate Guide to Peak Mental Performance at All Ages. Harper Collins Publishers.

Siegel, Kenneth M. Morris and Alan M. 1997. The Wall Street Journal Guide to Understanding Personal Finance. New York: Lightbulb Press, Inc. and Dow Jones & Co., Inc.

Tarokh L, Saletin JM, Carskadon MA. 2016. Sleep in adolescence: Physiology, cognition and mental health. Author Manuscript, Bethesda: Neurosci Biobehav Rev.

The Buffalo American. 1924. "Making Good at "The Tuskegee" United States Veterans' Hospital, No 91." October 30: 7.